A Journal of the American Civil War

GUEST EDITORS:
John M. Coski and Daniel F. Jasman, Jr.

MANAGING EDITOR:
David A. Woodbury

EDITORIAL CONSULTANT / PUBLISHER:
Theodore P. Savas

VOLUME FIVE   NUMBER ONE

Published quarterly by Regimental Studies, Inc., a nonprofit charitable corporation

STATEMENT OF PURPOSE: Regimental Studies, Inc., is a non-partisan, non-profit charitable corporation founded to further two specific goals. First, it is hoped that *Civil War Regiments* will encourage further research into the often neglected area of unit history studies by providing a serial outlet for that research. It is also our intent to raise funds for the preservation and protection of endangered Civil War sites by donating proceeds to various preservation organizations. To this end, your active support in the form of donations, advertisements, articles, and subscriptions, is both encouraged and welcomed. Thank you.

GENERAL INFORMATION

Civil War Regiments is published quarterly by Regimental Studies, Inc., a non-profit charitable corporation located at 1475 South Bascom Avenue, Suite 204, Campbell, CA 95008. Managing Editor: David A. Woodbury. Editorial Consultant/Publisher: Theodore P. Savas. Voice: (408) 879-9073. Facsimile: 408-879-9327. Toll-free order line: (800) 848-6585. The editorial department may be reached via electronic mail at 76710.261@compuserve.com.

Trade distribution is handled by Dick Frank at Stackpole Books, 5067 Ritter Road, Mechanicsburg, PA 17055-6921. (717) 796-0411 (phone); (717) 976-0412 (fax). Dealer inquires welcome.

SUBSCRIPTIONS, BACK ISSUES, COLLECTOR'S SETS

$29.95/year, ppd (four books), individual and institutional. Back issues may be ordered from the publisher. Write to Back Issues, CWR, 1475 South Bascom, Suite 204, Campbell, CA 95008, or call 1-800-848-6585, for pricing information and availability. Please specify the volume and issue number when placing your order. Prepayment with check, money order, or MC/V is required. Two hundred and fifty signed and numbered four-issue collector's sets for the premier volume were printed. Cost is $40.00 ppd. Inquire about availability. FOREIGN ORDERS: subscriptions (four issues) are $39.95/year, ppd. Payment in United States currency only, or MC/V. Books shipped surface mail. Allow eight to twelve weeks for delivery.

MANUSCRIPTS AND CORRESPONDENCE

We welcome manuscript inquiries. For author's guidelines, send a self-addressed, double-stamped business envelope to: Editor, *Civil War Regiments*, 1475 South Bascom, Suite 204, Campbell, CA 95008. Inquiries via electronic mail should be addressed to 76710.261@compuserve.com. Include a brief description of your proposed topic and the sources to be utilized. No unsolicited submissions will be returned without proper postage.

Book review inquiries or submissions should be directed to Dr. Archie McDonald, CWR Book Review Editor, Stephen F. Austin State University, Department of History, P.O. Box 6223, SFA Station, Nacogdoches, Texas 75962-6223. (409) 568-2407. Enclose a self-addressed-stamped-envelope if requesting a reply.

DONATIONS TO HISTORIC PRESERVATION PROJECTS

Thanks to your support, *Civil War Regiments* has been able to make a number of donations to Civil War-related preservation organizations. The recipients of these donations are listed below:

(LIFE MEMBER) ASSOCIATION FOR THE PRESERVATION OF CIVIL WAR SITES

RICHARD B. GARNETT MEMORIAL, HOLLYWOOD CEMETERY

HERITAGEPAC / CIVIL WAR ROUND TABLE ASSOCIATES

SAVE HISTORIC ANTIETAM FOUNDATION

TURNER ASHBY HOUSE, PORT REPUBLIC, VA

THE COKER HOUSE RESTORATION PROJECT, JACKSON, MS CWRT

AMERICAN BLUE & GRAY ASSOCIATION

APCWS 1993 MALVERN HILL/GLENDALE CAMPAIGN

THE C.S.S. HUNLEY PROJECT

This journal is printed on 50-lb. J.B. Offset recycled, acid-free paper.

COVER PHOTO: Confederate veterans outside the Confederate Museum (White House) in Richmond, at the 1907 U.C.V. reunion. Courtesy of the Cook Collection, Valentine Museum, Richmond, Virginia.

 A Journal of the American Civil War

THE MUSEUM OF THE CONFEDERACY

GUEST EDITORS / CONTRIBUTORS:

John M. Coski earned his Ph.D. from the College of William and Mary and has been Historian at The Museum of the Confederacy in Richmond, Virginia, since 1990. He is a past contributor to *Civil War Regiments* with an article on the 32nd Wisconsin Infantry, and is the author of the newly released book, *Capital Navy: The Men, Ships, and Operations of the James River Squadron* (Savas Woodbury Publishers, 1996).

Daniel F. Jasman, Jr., earned his B.A. in History and M.A. in Education from Virginia Commonwealth University. He worked as an intern at The Museum of the Confederacy from 1993-1995.

Introduction

The most valuable sources for historians studying Confederate and Federal units are accounts written by the soldiers themselves. Consistent with the mission of Regimental Studies, Inc., and with The Museum of the Confederacy's continuing effort to make its collections accessible to the public, this issue of *Civil War Regiments* features previously unpublished materials from the Museum's rich manuscript collections. Selected for publication from the thousands of letters and dozens of diaries are manuscript groups which offer extraordinary details on the histories of three Confederate regiments. One of those units, the Washington Artillery of New Orleans, is very familiar to historians. The others, the 14th Tennessee Infantry and 40th Georgia Infantry, have not received the attention they deserve.

Sergeant Robert Theodore Mockbee set out to compile and publish a history of the 14th Tennessee Infantry, Archer's Brigade, Army of Northern Virginia. In about 1910, Mockbee, Capt. June Kimble and Brig. Gen. William McComb began recording their own memories and soliciting papers from other survivors of the regiment. Kimble and McComb published a few articles in *Confederate Veteran,* but the aging men failed to produce a comprehensive regimental history. Mockbee in 1912 wrote a 65-page handwritten "Historical Sketch" of the 14th Tennessee Infantry. Eighty-three years later, Mockbee's "Historical Sketch" is published at last. Sensitive to the regiment's place in history, Mockbee wrote especially vivid descriptions of its role at Gaines' Mill, Second Manassas, Fredericksburg, Chancellorsville, Gettysburg, Falling Waters, and the Wilderness.

In contrast to the 14th Tennessee veterans, Maj. Raleigh Camp began to compile his memoir of the 40th Georgia in 1863. By the time of his death in 1867, he had written a narrative of the unit's first year of service and compiled a series of letters describing the subsequent campaign and siege of Vicksburg. Those letters are published here in their entirety, along with an introduction summarizing Camp's narrative of the 40th Georgia's first year. The only published memoir of the 40th Georgia deals almost exclusively with the 1864 Atlanta Campaign, so Camp's papers (only recently donated to the Museum) represent the first detailed history of a unit which saw substantial action in the Army of Tennessee.

"In the Field and on the Town with the Washington Artillery" is a chronological collection of letters and diary entries by members of that famed unit. William Miller Owen, in his classic *In Camp and Battle with the Washington Artillery,* made only cursory use of his brother Edward's 1863-1864 diary. Lieutenant Edward Owen recorded accounts of Chancellorsville and Gettysburg, along with gossipy details about his social life in Richmond and Petersburg. In contrast, the entries in Capt. John B. Richardson's 1861-1862 diary offer a sober daily record of weather and troop movements. Letters, mostly written in 1861-1862 and 1864-1865 by Lt. Edward ("Ned") Apps and Cpl. Fred A. Brode, describe life in camp and are a window on the mood of men whose homes were behind enemy lines. Students of the war will find the story of these documents familiar, but the perspectives will be entirely new.

John Coski
The Museum of the Confederacy

Regimental History Research Resources
at The Museum of the Confederacy

Sgt. Robert T. Mockbee's history of the 14th Tennessee Infantry, Maj. Raleigh Camp's account of the 40th Georgia Infantry in the Vicksburg campaign and the Washington Artillery documents exemplify the resources available at The Museum of the Confederacy for regimental history researchers. The Museum's Eleanor S. Brockenbrough Library houses letters, diaries, reminiscences, muster rolls, order books, newspapers, scrapbooks, hospital and cemetery records and other documents which shed light on scores of Confederate regiments and companies. The library also houses cased images, carte-de-visites, maps, pamphlets and Confederate imprints.

The richness of the Museum's collection owes in large part to its origins. Founded in 1890 to rescue the Confederate Executive Mansion from impending destruction, the Museum's governing body, the Confederate Memorial Literary Society, also made the collection of documents and books one of its chief objectives. By the time it opened to the public on February 22, 1986, the Museum was already the repository for the Mary DeRenne and the Southern Historical Society manuscript collections, and had received letters and diaries directly from Confederate veterans and their families and official and unofficial unit records from their former officers. So great was the prestige of the Museum's document collections that a young Johns Hopkins University historian, Dr. Douglas Southall Freeman, spent a few months in 1907 analyzing them and publishing a guide entitled *The Calendar of Confederate State Papers.* Today, in its centennial year, the Museum continues to receive valuable manuscripts.

The Brockenbrough Library and its resources are open to researchers, but under specific conditions. Library space and staff are limited, **so it is absolutely necessary to call or inquire in writing about the availability of information and to make an appointment.** The library is open 9:00 a.m. to 4:30 p.m. Monday through Friday. There is a modest fee to use the library and a handling fee for detailed mail requests (those beyond simple inquiries about library holdings). Photocopies are $.25 per page. Some items, particularly maps, original muster rolls, and fragile bound volumes cannot be photocopied. The library does not house service or pension records for Confederate soldiers and veterans. *Confederate Veteran* magazine (old series), *Southern Historical Society Papers,* the *Official Records* and other published sources vital to regimental history research are available at the library, but researchers are urged use those sources at city or university libraries, to which public access is easier.

Listed below by state and unit is a sampling of the documents most relevant to regimental research. In addition to the specific regimental sources, headquarters papers for the Department of Georgia and South Carolina, for such commanders as P.G.T. Beauregard, Henry Clayton, Roswell Ripley and Carter Stevenson, and staff officers as Archer Anderson and J.W. Ratchford contain a wealth of statistical and logistical information about units in those commands. The plurality of sources in the Museum's collections relate to Virginia units; those sources are, in fact, too voluminous to list here. Anyone conducting research on Virginia units should contact the Museum library to learn what items are in the collection. Most of the non-Virginia regimental resources are official muster rolls and unofficial rosters (sometimes descriptive) of companies and regiments, diaries and collections of letters.

ALABAMA

Clayton Guards: roll of officers and privates, March 30, 1861; sketch of company

Huntsville Guards: typed roster

20th Battalion, Light Artillery: morning reports, December 1863-February 1864

20th Battalion, Light Artillery: abstract of men who reenlisted
    for war, March 1864

1st Cavalry, Co. E: sketch in scrapbook

5th Cavalry: orders from Gen. Phillip D. Roddey, 1864-1865

8th Alabama Cavalry, Co. A: typescript roll

15th Cavalry, Co. E: muster roll

3rd Infantry, Co. A (Mobile Cadets): December 26, 1860 letter
    from Alphonso du Mont

3rd Infantry, Co. I (Wetumpka Light Guards): typescript of roll

4th Infantry: memorial of Ensign Hugh Lawson

4th Infantry, Co. I (North Alabamians): typed roster

4th Infantry: postwar list of officers and abstract of wartime ser-
    vice

5th Infantry: original muster rolls for all companies, February -
    October 1862

5th Battalion, Infantry: reports of the Battle of Chancellorsville

9th Infantry, Co. G: clipping of roll written from memory
    (1905)

10th Infantry, Co. D: typewritten roster

16th Infantry: letter book of Col. William B. Wood, October
    1861-January 1862

18th Infantry, Co. K: diary of Pvt. James M. Lanning, 1863

20th Infantry: letters of Sgt. William Woods, 1862-1864

22nd Infantry, Co. H (Sam Cooper Rifles): roll

23rd Infantry: roster of men who reenlisted for war, March
    1864

25th Infantry, Co. G: diary of Pvt. James M. Lanning,
    September 1864-March 1865

30th Infantry: report of the Battle of Missionary Ridge

33rd Infantry, Co. B: reminiscence by W.E. Mathews

38th Infantry: roll of field, staff and band, 1864-1865

38th Infantry, Co. D: descriptive list and account of pay, cloth-
    ing, etc., 1863, 1864

39th Infantry: reports of battles of Atlanta and Ezra Church,
    July 22 and 28, 1864

42nd Infantry, Co. D: account of battle of Resaca

43rd Infantry, Co. G: day book, descriptive lists, morning re-
    ports, December 1862-May 1864

47th Infantry: report of casualties at Cedar Mountain

47th Infantry: postwar list of officers and abstract of wartime
service

50th Alabama Infantry, Co. F: typescript list of veterans

56th Infantry: Alabama Band Concert program, March 27,
1865

Battle's Brigade (3rd, 5th, 6th, 12th and 26th Infantry):
monthly reports, April and October, 1864

Brantley's Brigade (22nd, 24th and 37th Infantry): roster of
officers, May 2, 1865

ARKANSAS

2nd Cavalry: papers of Col. William F. Slemons, April 1861-May
1865

Capt. A.V. Reever's Company, Washington County: roll
published in newspaper

3rd Infantry: list of officers (in Taliaferro's brigade),
November 1861

3rd Infantry: list of commissioned officers; typescript bounty
list of Co. H

3rd Infantry: original muster rolls of Companies E, H, and I,
1861-1862

FLORIDA

Ancilla Troopers: account of presentation of flag by ladies of
Sandy Ford

2nd Infantry: muster rolls of all companies, January-April 1863

3rd Infantry, Co. B: muster rolls, 1861, 1862, January 1863

3rd Infantry, Co. B: diary of Sgt. Edward C. Brush, March-May,
October-November 1862

3rd Infantry, Co. D: account book of Capt. John Inglis; letters
of John Inglis, 1864

3rd Infantry, Co. G: letters of Archie, Albert, Theodore and
John Livingston, 1862-1865

3rd Infantry: return, November 1, 1861

4th Infantry: return, November 21, 1861

8th Infantry, Co. C: muster rolls, May-June 1862

8th Infantry: postwar list of officers and abstract of wartime service

9th Infantry, Co. D: muster roll, May 1862

Letterbook, Headquarters of Military District of Florida, 1864-1865

Monthly reports, Department of Middle Florida, December 1861, January 1862

Field and Staff officers in Military Department of Middle and East Florida, March 4, 1862

GEORGIA

Savannah area local defense troops: diary of engineer Albert L. West, December 1864

2nd Battalion Cavalry; 4th, 7th and 27th Battalion Infantry; 38th and 39th Regiments Infantry: original returns, February 1862

2nd Infantry: report of public property lost upon falling back from Manassas, April 1, 1862

4th Infantry, Co. E ("Albany Guards"): roll from postwar newspaper clipping

5th Infantry, Co. C: resolutions on death of Sgt. Edward Hugh Hall

31st Infantry, Co. C ("Mitchell Guards"): roll and article from February 1862 Rome, Georgia, newspaper

1st Regiment: list of commissioned officers (in Taliaferro's brigade), November 1861

Capt. John P. W. Read's battery (10th Regiment, Co. K): roll published in newspaper, 1862

Chestalu Light Artillery (38th Regiment Volunteers): muster roll, 1864

12th Infantry, Co. D: typed roll

16th Infantry: diary and letterbook of surgeon, Lt. Robert Poole Myers, 1862-1865

40th Infantry: letters of Maj. Raleigh S. Camp, 1863-1865; account (ca. 1866) of Vicksburg Campaign

46th Infantry: quartermaster requisitions, September 1862

48th Infantry: roster, March 28, 1862

49th Infantry: roll of soldiers on duty, October-December 1864; guard report (March 27-28, 1862); list of casualties from battle of Johns Farm, March 25, 1865

49th Infantry, Companies G and I: casualties at Gettysburg

51st Infantry: roster of officers, April 16, 1862

61st Infantry, Co. I (Thompson Guards): muster roll and casualty list

Toomb's/Benning's Brigade (1st, 2nd, 3rd, 10th, 17th, 20th, 24th and 38th Infantry): postwar lists of officers and abstracts of wartime service

Sorrel's Brigade, formerly Wright's Brigade (3rd, 22nd, 48th, 64th Infantry regiments and 2nd and 10th Infantry battalions): diary of Gen. G. Moxley Sorrel [consisting mostly of field maps], April-November 1864

Cummings' Brigade (34th, 36th, 39th and 56th Infantry): returns, lists of officers, reports of casualties, deserters, shoemakers, masons and mechanics, and other papers, October 1863-March 1864

Military District of Georgia: headquarters papers of Brig. Gen. A. R. Lawton, 1861-1862

2nd Military District, Department of Georgia: headquarters papers of Brig. Gen. H. W. Mercer, 1862

KENTUCKY

2nd Infantry: memorial of Ensign Robert Clinton Anderson

LOUISIANA

2nd Infantry (Stark's) Brigade: roster of officers, 1862

1st Infantry Regiment: roster of officers, 1862

1st Infantry Regiment: list of sick, November 6, 1861

1st Infantry Battalion: special orders, Army of the Peninsula, March 1862

2nd Infantry Regiment: roster, 1862

4th Battalion: return, February 1862

6th Infantry, Company F: muster rolls, December 1861-October 1862

9th Infantry: order book, 1861-1862; general order book, 1862-1864

9th Infantry, Co. B: muster roll

13th Infantry: typed sketch of Capt. Howard C. Wright

14th Infantry: roster of commissioned officers, 1862

15th Infantry: roster of commissioned officers, 1862

List of Louisiana volunteers deceased or discharged as of August 31, 1862

MARYLAND

1st Battery: report by Capt. J. P. Crane on battle of Gettysburg

3rd Battery: condensed diary of Capt. William L. Ritter, 1861-
1865

4th Artillery, Chesapeake Battery: partial (postwar) list

Co. B, Light Infantry, Maryland Guard: photocopy of descriptive list

1st Battalion, Co. H: clothing list for non-commissioned officers, October-December 1863

Winder Guard: record of deserters, 1863

MISSISSIPPI

15th Infantry, Co. F (Water Valley Rifles): roll upon organization

19th Infantry: report of Battle of Gettysburg

29th Infantry, Co. C: roll book, April 26, 1865

31st Infantry: reminiscences by Col. M.D. Stephens

34th Infantry, Co. B: typescript prison diary of Sgt. Lafayette
Rogan, 1864

39th Infantry, Co. I: morning reports, August 20, 30, 1862

Featherstone's Brigade (13th, 17th, 18th and 21st Infantry):
postwar list of officers and abstract of service

MISSOURI

5th Infantry, Co. E: roster recorded from memory, 1876

10th Infantry, Co. E: muster rolls, 1865

NORTH CAROLINA

North Carolina Reserves (1st, 2nd and 3rd battalions): reports
of sick

Cape Fear Artillery, Co. K: muster roll, June-August 1862

Fayetteville Independent Light Artillery: 1929 newspaper article

2nd Cavalry (19th Regiment), Co. C: diary of Pvt. John W.
Gordon, 1864-1865

1st Infantry, Co. A (Edgecombe Guards): roster

1st Battalion Sharpshooters: muster rolls, September-
December 1864

3rd Infantry: report of action at Gettysburg

4th Infantry, Co. A: two letters from R. P. Allen, July-August 1864

4th Infantry, Co. E: muster rolls, December 1862-April 1863

5th Infantry, Co. E: memorandum book and notes of Capt. Speight Brock West

6th Infantry: postwar list of officers and abstract of wartime service

13th Infantry, Cos. A-K, muster rolls, April-June 1863

16th Infantry, Cos. B-M, F&S, muster rolls, April -June 1863

21st Infantry: orders and lists of wounded

23rd Infantry, Co. B: muster roll, March-April 1862

24th Infantry, Co. E: memories of specific campaigns by C.S. Powell

27th Infantry, Co. F: typescript of diary of Corp. Joseph Mullen, Jr., May 1864-May 1865

28th Infantry, Co. I: roll book

28th Infantry: officers' commissions and sundry documents

28th Infantry, Co. I: diary of Sgt. G.B. Harding, May-June 1864

32nd Infantry, Co. E: copy of diary of Capt. Gilbert M. Sherrill

34th Infantry: typed copy of 1863 letter from D.C. Williams to wife

35th Infantry, Co. K: bounty roll, March 1862

37th Infantry, Co. E: roll, brief history and sundry documents by Martin Van Buren Moore

38th Infantry: consolidated provision returns, 1862

46th Infantry, Co. K: original roll book

52nd Infantry, Cos. A, B, C, H: muster rolls, January-June 1864

67th Infantry, Co. A: muster rolls, October 1863-February 1864

Daniel's Brigade (32nd, 43rd, 45th and 53rd Infantry, 2nd Battalion Infantry): field returns, September 9, 1863, October 31, 1863, April 9, 1864

Iverson's/Ramseur's Brigade (5th, 12th, 20th and 23rd Infantry): field returns, September 9, 1863, April 9, 1864

Hoke's division: letters, circulars and orders, 1862-1865

Typed index of companies by county of origin

SOUTH CAROLINA

Palmetto Battalion Light Artillery: returns, July and August 1862; report on organization and activities, 1862

Pee Dee Artillery ("Darlington Guards"): history by Col. David Gregg McIntosh

1st Artillery: memorial from Miss Claudine Rhett

2nd Artillery: copies of transcripts of letters from Walter D. Spann, 1864

Barnwell Dragoons: return, June 19, 1862

Hardwicke's Mounted Rifles: morning report, June 15, 1862

Marion Mounted Men of Combahee: several reports and papers, May-July 1862

Rutledge Mounted Riflemen: report on skirmish at Pocataligo, May 29, 1862

2nd Battalion Cavalry: returns, July and October 1862

4th Cavalry, Co. D: diary of Capt. Thomas Pinckney, May-December 1864

4th Cavalry, Co. I: diary of D.E. Gordon

6th Cavalry, Co. I: morning report book, 1864-1865; descriptive list of horses

Cherokee Ponds Guard: roll

Edgefield Riflemen: roll and description of flag

Holcombe Legion: list of marksmen, May 31, 1862; undated field return

1st, 2nd, 3rd, 5th, 6th, 7th, 8th, 15th and 20th Infantry: lists of officers and abstracts of wartime service

1st Infantry, Co. A (Edisto Rifles): descriptive roll and records

2nd Regiment (Palmetto Guard): diary of Sgt.George M. Lalane, 1861-1862, 1864

12th Infantry: consolidated provision record

14th Infantry, Co. D: roll

17th Infantry: in memorium of Pvt. John Cunningham

20th, 22nd and 23rd, 24th and 25th Infantry: lists of marksmen

21st Infantry, Co. A: reminiscences of Sam Hathaway

22nd, 24th and 25th Infantry: casualties of battle on James Island, June 16, 1862

25th Infantry, Co. F: record book

25th Infantry (Eutaw Regiment), Co. E: diary of Lt. George M. Lalane, 1864-1865

Siege Train, Co. A: muster rolls, December 1864-February 1865

Provisional Forces: letter book of Col. Richard H. Anderson, 1861-1862

Military Districts of South Carolina, 1-6: roster of officers, spring 1862

TENNESSEE

17th, 23rd, 25th, and 44th Infantry: "Black list of men who were noted for cowardice, etc. at battles of Murfreesboro, November 30-December 1, 1862

18th, 26th, 32nd and 45th Infantry: report of casualties from Battle of Missionary Ridge

48th Infantry, Co. E: diary of Lt. James E. Mackey, December 1861-January 1865

TEXAS

Capt. M. J. Kirk's company of Partisan Rangers: return, October 1862

1st, 4th and 5th Infantry: postwar list of officers and abstract of service

4th Infantry, Co. I (Navarro Rifles): diary of Sgt. Robert G. Holloway, 1861-1862

15th (Consolidated), 17th and 31st dismounted cavalry and Merrick's Battalion: original returns and rosters, Camp Rogers, Texas, April 1865

"the Sun never Shined on a braver
& truer Set of Soldiers":

The 14th Tennessee Infantry Regiment[1]

SGT. ROBERT T. MOCKBEE

EDITOR'S NOTE: After four years of actual war, the veterans of South and North girded themselves for the much longer struggle fought over the interpretation of the events of 1861-1865—a struggle which occurred as much among veterans of each army as between old foes. In the post-bellum struggle among Confederate units for credit and glory, few commands labored harder than the men of the 14th Tennessee Infantry, of Archer's Tennessee Brigade, Army of Northern Virginia. The unit's bloodiest fights and greatest sacrifices were made in battles in which they were overshadowed by other commands: by Hood's Texas (and Georgia) Brigade at Gaines' Mill and by Pickett's Virginia Division on the third day of Gettysburg. In the latter battle, wrote the 14th's Capt. June Kimble, Archer's Brigade "led the advance, was the first to enter the enemy's works and the last to quit those works. . . ."[2] At Gaines' Mill, the Tennesseeans made an unsuccessful charge on the Federal position which some claimed created the "diversion" which allowed Hood's Texans to carry the position and win their place in military legend.[3]

    While the Tennesseeans were not shy in writing articles and delivering speeches staking their own claim to military glory, none of them published full-length memoirs or histories of the regiment.[4] Only recently has a modern historian written a partial history of the regiment.[5] At the beginning of the century, a few veterans of the regiment amassed recollections and deposited them at the Confederate Museum, now The Museum of the Confederacy. June Kimble, who published an account of Archer's Brigade at Gettysburg in *Confederate Veteran*, contributed several of his own papers (rosters and accounts of Company A) and papers he solicited from comrades regarding the regiment's participation at Chancellorsville and Gettysburg. R. E. McCulloch contributed a brief regimental history.

Instrumental in accumulating documents and reminiscences at the museum was the regiment's long-time commander, William McComb. The Pennsylvania-born McComb had moved to Clarksville in the 1850s. He enlisted as a private in the 14th Tennessee, was elected second lieutenant in May 1861 and rose quickly to command of the regiment after Second Manassas, then became brigadier general in 1865. After the war, McComb married and settled in his wife's home in Louisa County, Virginia. Following her death in 1895, McComb spent much of his time in Richmond and became a booster of the nascent Confederate Museum.[6] In addition to writing a 14-page recollection of the brigade's campaigns in 1864-1865, McComb also encouraged his comrades to contribute their memoirs and papers to the museum.[7]

Most notable among the papers submitted was a lengthy (65 pages of legal-size paper) handwritten narrative by Sgt. Robert Theodore Mockbee, of Company B. McComb deposited Mockbee's "Historical Sketch" at the Museum in 1912 with the qualified endorsement that he had "looked over" the paper and "find the different Sketches very accurate and worthy in a place of history. My eyes are failing and it is impossible for me to review it as Carefully as I would like to do. But I hope Some one more Competent Some day may arrange the paper properly." A year earlier, McComb had furnished to Mockbee his "recollections of what our gallant and noble boys went through from January 1, 1864 to the Surrender at Appomattox April 9th 1865." The general encouraged his "dear friend and Comrade" to continue his work until he "can get a pretty full account of the part the 14th Tenn. Regt. took in the A. of N. Virginia[.] We made a record we need not be ashamed of having published to the world."

Published here—83 years later, is Mockbee's full "Sketch." It is printed as it was written, including errors in spelling and capitalization; "[sic.]" is used only when the reader would be likely to mistake a spelling error for a typographical error. Mockbee was consistent in several such errors (which have not been marked in the text), most notably inverting the vowels in such words as "their" and "field," and misspelling lieutenant as "liutenant." His capitalization in words beginning with "A" and "C" is difficult to discern. To allow publication of

Mockbee's entire history, the editors have chosen not to identify every person, place and event mentioned, but to annotate it only with occasional notes from other documents in the museum's collection.

Historical Sketch of the 14th Tenn Regt of Infantry C.S.A. 1861-1865

by Sgt. R. T. Mockbee

Robert Theodore Mockbee was born in Stewart County, Tennessee, on August 16, 1841. Mockbee's family owned no land and no slaves. According to his response to the Tennessee veterans questionnaire, Mockbee worked before the war as a brick mason, a farmer "or anything my hands could do." He enlisted in the 14th Tennessee Infantry as a sergeant, served in the regiment at that rank throughout the war and was discharged at Appomattox. After the war, he married a South Carolina woman whom he had met during the war, and lived in South Carolina from 1866 to 1893, when he moved to Arkansas, then to Memphis. He described the Reconstruction era as "more trying than any of the experiences of the war." A devoted follower of the "Straightout White Mans Democratic Ticket," Mockbee served four years as a representative of Chester County in the South Carolina legislature.[8]

The Fourteenth Tenn Regiment of Infantry Volunteers Was Composed of Eleven Companies as follows Company (A) Capt W.A. Forbes, (Co B) Capt M.G. Gholston (Co H) Capt F.S. Beaumont (Co G) Capt I Brunson (Co K) Capt J. W. Lockert (Co L) Capt Ed Hewit, all from Montgomery County. (Co. D.) Capt. H. C. Buckner (Co E) Capt Clay Roberts and (Co F) Capt W. E. Lowe from Stewart County. (Co. C.) Capt. W. Lowe and (Co I) Capt W.P. Simmons, From Robertson Co, the above names were the Captains of each Company as mentioned above were those in command when companies first assembled at "Camp Duncan" (the Fair Grounds near Clarksville, Montgomery County Tenn.) and were organized into a Regimental by the Election of Regimental feild and Staff officers as follows W.A. Forbes Colonel, M.G. Gholson Liut. Col and N. Brandon: Major. W.W. Thompson Adjutant, Sergt-Major Dr. J F Johnson Surgeon Dr. J.B. Martin Asst Surgeon, A.J. Allensworth Q.M. G. H. Martin Commissary; Johnson Goostree Commissary Sergt. The Regiment was Mustered into service for the term of one year by Genl W.A. Quarles on May 17th 1861. And soon thereafter moved to Camp Quarles near Hamptons Spring, some miles further from Clarksville Near the Kentucky line. The time until late in June was spent in drilling and becoming familiar with the duties of a soldier, and to the thourgher trainning given by Col Forbes, and Adjutant Thompson ably assisted by the Company officers, Was due much of the efficiency afterwards displayed on Many occasions during thier experience as soldiers under Lee, Jackson, and A.P. Hill and so thanked was that efficiency shown that on more than one occasion it drew from those Commanders words of hearty commendation.

It was while in Camp of instruction that by an act of the Legislative of Tenn the question of Secession was submitted to a vote of the People of the state and Volunteer soldiers then enlisted in the service of the state were permitted. and many of the young soldiers cast thier first Ballots in favor of Seperation and

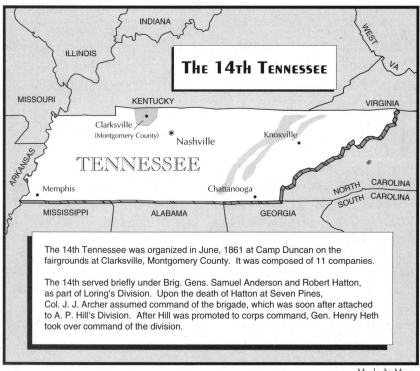

THE 14TH TENNESSEE

The 14th Tennessee was organized in June, 1861 at Camp Duncan on the fairgrounds at Clarksville, Montgomery County. It was composed of 11 companies.

The 14th served briefly under Brig. Gens. Samuel Anderson and Robert Hatton, as part of Loring's Division. Upon the death of Hatton at Seven Pines, Col. J. J. Archer assumed command of the brigade, which was soon after attached to A. P. Hill's Division. After Hill was promoted to corps command, Gen. Henry Heth took over command of the division.

Mark A. Moore

representation in the Confederate Government already formed at Montgomery Alabama.

About — June the Regt was ordered to Nashville.[9] Many of the men were sick in camp or at home on sick leave, measles having broken out and fully one third of some companies were sick. When the Regiment reached Nashville they were ordered to proceed at once to Virginia to the great delight of the Men, Most of whom feared that the great impending battle would be fought; our Independence gained and the War ended without the Regiment having an opportunity to fire a gun. the same feeling was had to a greater extent by the many sick men left behind, for they fully expected after it was known that the Regt had been ordered to Virginia that if they did get to the scene of active Opperations Col Forbes and the Fourteenth would just put the finishing touches to McDowells army then advancing on "Beauregard" at Manassas and when on July the 21st the news was flashed over the country that the long looked for battle was being fought; and later that a great victory had been won, sick men forgot the "Measles" and heedless of warning from home folks and Doctor alike more than forty of the poor shaddows of men whos legs fairly wabled as they walked, boarded the Mid night train under the cane and command of Liut David Martin of (Co B)and started. hopeing that they might at least reach and see the feild where southern valor had put the flight the northern host. Not doubting at first that "Col Forbes" and the Fourteenth had been in at the death; and we would be able to venture home with the Regiment and listen to the Peans of praise bestowed upon the "conquering heros."

But alas after a stay of some days at Bristol Tenn.[10] and there the poor measly crowd overtook them, and learned that they had gained no glory only been taking the rain which seemed incessant and were a disabled set as compared with the gay and festive body of men that had bidden farewell to thier loved ones and thier native section to join thier fortresses with those of comrades from all sections of the south already assembled under "Beauregard" and "Johnston" on the soil of Virginia.

Nothwithstanding this as they soon learned by experience which was only a very slight foretaste of what was in store for us in the not distant future. The men had in some measure taken on that jolly good spirit that was ever the characteristic of the Confederate soldier and could sing "Let the wide world was as it will well be gay and happy still."

THE FIRST SIGHT OF GENL LEE[11]

After a few days bivuaced at dear old Lynchburg, the Regiment with others from Tennessee were ordered to board the trains and was slowly transported to Staunton Va. where we disembarked And there for the first time many of the men looked upon the face and form of the Man who was afterwards to take his place among the greatest military Leaders the world ever produced. Genl R. E. Lee had been assigned to the command of the department of what was known as North West Va. And he commenced at once to organize the trooops for active service.

FIRST BRIGADE ORGANIZATION

The Fourteenth Was placed in a Brigade with Col Manneys 1st Tenn Regt and Col Robert Hatton's 7th Tenn Regt the Brigade was placed under command of Brig Genl Saml Anderson of Nashville; who had served in the War with Mexico, as Col or Liut Col. of a Tenn Regt.[12]

After a short stay at Staunton the amy was moved by Rail to "Millboro" on the Chesapeake & Ohio Rail Road. And from there commenced our first real march on one of the hottest Augt days ever experienced by the writer. The Line of March led across the Warm Springs Mountain to the Great Watering place "Warm Springs"; And the road assecending the Mountain by easy grades led through a section entirely destitute of Water. before the summit was reached all the water in canteens was exhausted and the men exhausted by the miles of continuous uphill march; and extream heat who had started out in regular military order in Column of fours; were now scattered along the road for miles. Many of them having sought the friendly shade afforded by the trees on the roadside and when in the late afternoon the summit was reached by those in advance there was presented to there view such a grand Panorama of Nature that the heat, thirst, and fatigue of that terable march was for the time forgotten in the contemplation of one of the finest to be had in all that section. in front as far as the eye could reach arose the great ranges of the Aleghaney Mountains rising one above the other until the highest peaks seemed lost in the sky. And just beneath (as it seemed at first— only a mile or two) lay the beautiful Warm Springs Valley; With its feilds of wavering Grain, green pastures, with herds of fat cattle grazing; and the cozy farm houses nestling in the shady groves; With the courses of many rippling brooks marking thier way from the springs across feilds and wood to the main stream that naturally drained the valley; And like a gem as a setting to the veiw, Was the village of Warm Springs, the great Hotel, surrounded by the bath & spring houses and many other buildings;

It was only for a few minutes that Nature and the sight of the flowing streams in the Valley below called the wearied straglers to Move on, and the Mad rush in which it was hard to control the now weak and wabling legs of the thoroughly disorganized mob, driven by a raging thirst to reach the water they had glimpses of in the valley below. And it seemed to those who were thus urged on that the distance was interminable, and as it proved to be instead of a mile or so down that winding road it was six or eight miles. At last the goal was reached and it was all the officers and More thoughtful men could do to restrain the famished men from drinking too much Water, and with all the warning many were made sick. a day or two of rest was nescessary to enable the command to proceed on the march to Huntersville in Pochahontas County. The march led through a comparetively unsettled wooded country though we were glad to find it well watered. We camped for a day or so at "Gatewoods" large farm one of the finest in all that section and the owner Col. Gatewood was an ardent southern man and mainfested it in his kind treatment of our officers and men something that could not be said of every man to be met in this section of Virginia at that time and which became a separate state during the war on account of the Union sentiment that prevailed.

Huntersville was reached and the command was placed in camp to allow the army to gather; and the line of supply trains were formed to haul supplies from Millboro to Huntersville which was made a base from which they were to be distributed as the advance of the army which might require or need.

CAMP LIFE AT HUNTERSVILLE

The time of the "Fourteenth" was largely taken up in the routine of guard duty and daily Drilling, Morning & afternoon. the intervals being given to such sport and recreation as could be thought of or devised by those so inclined Mostly it was of an inocent nature But the gameing habit to some extent became prevalent, and it was common to see groups around some man dealing "Chuck a Luck" and other playing cards for money. there was in most of the companies one or more who played on the violin, and at night could be heard the notes of the fiddle, and the call of the prompter, as the mazes of a "cotilion" were gone through or the old "Virginia Reel" for a variation. The lady partner in the dance was distinguished by a handkerchief (not always <u>white</u>) tied around the right arm. in those "Stag Dances" the men conducted themselves with all the grace of a "Chesterfeild" toward thier "so-called Lady partners.["] Which was returned by the "Ladies" going through with all the delightful curtsy and graceful Movements as the figures of the dance were called; that Many of the boys remembered as having been taught by "Dan Gordon" and "Col Bob Saucy" in various neighborhoods in Montgomery and adjoining counties of Middle Tenn– Where they had taught the young people how to "trip the light-fantastic toe"

After a comparetively pleasant stay of a week or more we marched across Elk Mountain to Big Spring, and Valley Mountain where we camped for probably twenty days in the very midts of the Aleghany Mountains and and for a month it seemed to rain as it must have done in the "days of Noah" down in the deep valley when we were surrounded by mountains on all sides. at times the sun would be shining without a cloud to be seen. And before we could realize that it was possible clouds would roll over the mountains tops and deluge of water come down that threatened to devastate the entire encampment and to add to our discomfort the nights were extremely cold, while the heat of the sun between showers was something feirce indeed. The result of this weather was the beginning of the terible Epidemic of Mountain fever which prevailed in the entire army and was especially severe in the Fourteenth Tenn Regt Many cases developing into an agravated

Type of Typhoid fever of many of the men died.

Early in September Genl Lee made an in effective effort to surprise the Federal force holding a strong by fortified positions on Cheat Mountain, and after a long and wearisome march through tangled undergrowth over mountains without roads, with no artillery and the men with only three days rations returned to camp at "Mingo Flats."[13] Worn out, and scores of them with scortching fever burning out thier very vitals, and to add to the already bad state of affairs the inefficiency of the medical department espescially in the 14th Tenn Regt. was apparent to evry one; With no addequate supply of Ambulances to transport the hourly increasing number of sick and helpless men. The ordinary wagons used for hauling supplies from Huntersville were made use of to Move the sick over the now almost impassible mountain roads, which greatly added to the sufferings of the fever stricken men, and many of them were beyond the hope of receovering when they reached "Camp Edna" at the eastern side of Elk Mountain where the Brigade was ordered into camp. the graves of between thirty and forty of the men of the Fourteenth tells of the fatality of the dread disease and besides many others who had been carried on to Warm and Hot Springs where the large hotels had been turned into Hospitals for the care of the hundreds of sick many of whom died. and those poor men as truly gave thier lives for thier country as those who afterwards yeilded thirs on the many battlefeilds of Va[14]

One of the worst features connected with the terrible state of affairs was the almost total enefficiency of the medical department. This compiled with the wanton neglect on the part of some of those in charge of it aggravated and made worse the conditions by which we were surrounded. one single instance of the many that came to light, will suffice to show. One surgeon of a Regiment whose unfortunate desire and tastes for drink led him to appropriate to his own use the scant supply of spirits furnished for the use of the sick. and day by day he was in an almost maudlin state of drunkeness. Fortunately for the good of the service this party who shamefully disgraced his Proffession soon resigned, and his place was filled by one who came up to the full measure of responsibility the position demanded.

Soon after the Regiment went into camp at "Edna" Genl Lee

with the greater portion of his army marched to the assistance of Genl Floyd at Big Sewell Mountain leaving the 1st Regt the 14th and probably the 7th Regt at "Camp Edna."

THE FIRST WINTER QUARTERS BUILT

The short campaign of Genl Lee against the Federals under Rozencrans in the Kanawa Valley soon ended without any serious fighting or results at all advantageious to our army and the forces were ordered elsewhere and Genl Lee was sent to Charleston SC

Genl Loring being left in command of the forces near Huntersville. Late in the fall we were ordered to move beyond Huntersville where we camped and at once proceeded to built winter quarters. The cabins constructed by the "Fourteenth" were of logs with stick and mud chimneys, the cracks well lined with pine boards with roof of same weighted with poles to hold them in place.[15]

By this time the health of the men was greatly improved and the recieving of many boxes containing clothing and other nescessaries from loved ones at home made life in our new quarters much more pleasant. After the rainy season was over the weather was all that could be desired; and the people living near was able to supply our foragers with much that added to the regular rations made liveing almost luxurious so far as eating was concerned.

But all anticipations of spending the winter in our comfortable quarters was cut short about the 15 of December when orders came to get ready to move at once. And next day found us on the road marching towards the Shenandoah Valley by way of the Bath Allum Springs Road & Bridgwater. At Harrisonburg we struck the Valley Turnpike leading from Staunton to Winchester, and for the first time passed through that beautiful region afterwards made famous by Stonewall Jackson and his men. And our first Christmas was spent at Strausburg and much of the hilarity with which the days was always observed at home was in evidence. More or less "Apple Jack" had found its way into camp and not a few water-buckets full of "Egg Nog" was dispensed by the different messes: and in many instances Turkey was indulged in at dinner through the provident foresight of foragers sent out on the line of march on Christmas Eve, and the night following. like indulgences however were not enjoyed by many of the "Fourteenth" any other Christmas during the war.

The march was resumed the next day and we soon reached Winchester and "Lorings Division became a part of the Army under Command of Genl "Stonewall" Jackson. Romney Campaign.

After a few days in camp Genl Jackson on January 1st 1862 commenced his celebrated campaign in which the objective points were Hancock Maryland on the North bank of the Potomac River where a considerable force of the Enemy were , and "Romney" on the "South branch of the Potomac"

The first days march was through a beautiful country and the Spring like weather with the prospect of soon meeting the Enemy seemed to inspire our men to move with that alacrity that afterwards gained for them the "sobriquet" of "Foot Cavalry" We reached the vicinity of Berkley Springs Where the Enemy had an outpost of some strength consisting of Infantry & Artillery. We Bivuaced in a beautiful Valley covered with a grove of timber, beneath which; on piles of leaves our beds were made and with the stars shining brightly overhead the tired men found that sweet sleep that only comes to the weary on the bosom of dear old Mother earth.

But alas how things in nature change. When about early dawn next morning when order was passed to be ready to move at a moments notice and the blankets were thrown back a deluge of snow would fall in the faces of the partially aroused sleepers who found themselves with several inches of snow covering the ground and no fire to warm by; and then commenced our experiences of cold and exposure that made the "Romney" campaign ever memorable to the men engaged in it. All day the "Fourteenth Regt" stamped thier feet in the snow to keep from freezing almost in sight of where we slept the previous night and almost in view of the enemy at Berkley Springs. Genl Jackson was directing from near where we were the movements of other troops in an endeavor to cut of thier way of escape to Hancock Md: And late in the evening the federals discovering his plans hurriedly fled and Andersons Brigade was ordered to pursue the fugitives. We followed them closely but failed to overtake them as they plunged into the Icy waters of the "Potomac" and made thier escape by wading waist deep altho Ice was floating in the stream.[16]

The command was ordered into camp in a large feild surrounded by rail fences which we were ordered to use to make fires. On this day January 2nd 1862 near Berkley Springs some of the "Fourteenth" saw thier first of our men who were killed by the enemy. they were two members of a "Baltimore Company" who were in advance of our forces as we approached the "Springs" they had been left lying by the roadside on the snow by thier comrades who were in pursuit of the flying foe. and they were the only ones that we saw during this otherwise strenuous campaign of thirty days. The wagon trains having come up The Brigade went on to camp cleaning off the snow and getting straw from neighboring farms for beding. our condition was some what more pleasant on the 3d than on the night before with fence rails for beds in an open feild it was hard work to keep from freezing.

On the afternoon occured an incident worthy of note in connection with a member of (Co B) W.H. Frazier who had obtained a Transfer from (Co A) to (Co B) was sitting near the fire in front of his tent when a Rifle shell from the enemys guns across the River fell near the camp "Ricocheted" going through the Tent took Frazier a side swipe across the face and knocking him into the fire and but for the timely assistance of Liut T.W. Lewis he would have been badly burned. As it was he was badly stunned and the skin torn from his forehead so as to make it appear he was fatally wounded. the poor fellow though soon found his voice and lustily begged to be taken to his "Mother". it all resulted in Frazier getting a discharge as at that stage of the War the simple fact of a mans having been grazed by a "cannon Ball" was quite sufficient to insure an honorable discharge. It was afterwards told that Frazier went inside the lines and becoming involved in a difficulty with a Federal soldier at Hopkinsville Ky killed him and when arrested the plea of <u>insanity</u> was made as a result of his injury and he was turned loose.[17] At any rate the distinction belongs to (Co B) of having the first man struck by a misle from the enemy in the Fourteenth Tenn. Regt.

(ON TO ROMNEY)

After a few days spent in making Feints of trying to cross the river near "Hancock Md" Genl Jackson marched across the mountains towards "Romney" by way of Hanging Rock. where we saw the first evidences of that devlish spirit of maliscious mean and wanton distruction which afterwards brought devastation to the whole of the beautiful Shenandoah Valley. dwellings, barns and other buildings had been burned all along the road. When we arrived at Romney we found that "Genl Kelly" with a large force had hastily abandoned the place leaving quantitites of stores to fall into Genl Jacksons hands.

The Brigade of Genl Anderson was sent several miles down the South Branch of the Potomac and went into camp near a suspension Bridge on the "Moorefeild Pike". Where we did some strenuous Picket duty for several weeks. With snow and Ice six or eight inches deep all the time. Some of the men of the "Fourteenth" have in mind the comfortable cabins we had left near Huntersville proceeded to build again here, and others built chimneys to thier tent.

THE FIRST GRAY BACK

While here some of the men of the Fourteenth had an experience in the life of a soldier that is not mentioned in either Army Regulations or "Hardee's Tactics. When first placed on duty at the suspension Bridge as Pickets we found the bridge keepers house on the West side of the river had been occupied by the Federals as quarters for thier men on Picket there and we proceeded to use it too as quarters for the reserve force on duty. The Yanks had built bunks around the walls inside each large enough for two men to sleep in and had them filled with wheat straw. A large fireplace made it comfortable, and the men out on Picket post for more than a half mile down the Moorfeild Pike counted the slow passing minutes that would bring to an end thier lonely vigil of two hours duration, and with delight hasten back to the blazing log fire awaiting them at the Bridge, and after getting thoroughly thawed out, turn in on the nice straw bed vacated by those who relieved them.

But oh, horrors upon the return to camp next day after being relieved, it was soon discovered that evry man was poluted with vermin, better known in polite circles as "Graybacks" up to that time unknown to the men of the "Fourteenth" but afterwards the uncommon thing was not to have them. And some went so far as to quote "Genl Lee" as having said that it was a sure indication that a man was not much of a soldier who did not have them on him. However that is not the only thing attributed to "Genl Lee" that cannot be proven: but it was a good excuse for having to scratch.

While at this place the news came of the Battle of Fishing Creek a disaster to our arms and made worse by the death of Genl Zollicoffer a man much loved by evry Tennessean, and mourned by the whole South. And there arose especialy among the men and officers of "Lorings Division a spirit of discontent which was made worse by some of those in command of Regiments and Brigades harshly criticizing Genl Jackson conduct of the campaign in general; and went so far as to accuse him of undue favoritism in leaving Lorings Division to undergo the hardships and exposure incident to our nearness to the enemy which was made worse by the vigourous winter weather prevailing and taking his own old Brigade back to thier comfortable quarters at Winchester.

The Authorities at Richmond were appealed to by some whos envy or ambition was the leading motive and it went so far as to result in Genl Jackson tendering his resignation; which through the influence of those who knew and appreciated his great worth and ability fortunately succeeded in getting him to withdraw it.

In the last days of January we recieved orders to return to Winchester and marched through Romney at Sundown the evening we broke camp near the Bridge with orders to continue the march until the Wagon trains which had preceded us were overtaken. Some did so, but many sought shelter from the biting cold after a few miles in the farm houses or Barns, others built fires by the roadside, and waited till daylight to resume the wearisome march towards Winchester. Where we went into camp again. Many of the Fourteenth had sore and frostbitten feet to nurse while others were sent to the Hospitals from the exposure; and hard service of the thirty days campaign.

After a comparitively pleasant stay of some weeks at Winchester we were ordered to move and proceeded by way of Snicker Ferry across the Shanandoah River and across the Blue Ridge through Snickers Gap by way of the Aldie Pike to Mannassas where we took trains for Fredricksburg on our way to the mouth of Aquia Creek.

Where we relieved the Second Tenn- Col. Bates Regt which had been ordered to Tennessee to join the Western army under Genl A.S. Johnson. We remained only a short time here on the Potomac and went back to Fredricksburg and went into camp remaining there until ordered to join Genl J E Johnson at Yorktown on the Peninsula. We reached Yorktown, and found that McClellan was assembling a large force to move on Richmond from that direction.

While here the "Fourteenth" Reorganized by Electing Company and Feild officers and Enlisted for the War. Col. Forbes reelected Colonel, Capt G.A. Harrell Liut Col. and Liutenant Wm McComb Major.- there was many changes made in commisioned officers of the difirent companies. Many new men being promoted from the ranks and many who had held commissions before were left out and they almost without exception left the Regiment most of them going to the Western army.[18]

Soon after this Genl. Johnson commenced to retreat from before Yorktown and was closely followed by the Federals under McClellan, and on the morning of the second day commenced the Battle of Williamsburg. Andersons Tenn. Brigade now composed of the First (Turney), Seventh, and Fourteenth Regiments. (Manneys Regt- having been sent to the Western army).[19] While not actively participating witnessed much of the fighting which onlookers seemed to be without any important results to either side, unless it was to enable Genl Johnson to get his Artilery and trains safe on the road to Richmond, out of reach of the enemy.

On the next day occurred the Battle of West Point on the York River, where General Anderson led the Brigade <u>end fore most</u> in columns of fours through Hoods Texas Brigade that was formed in line of Battle across the Road and had engaged the Enemy (Co H) Capt J.J. Crusman commanding was immediately in front following Genl Anderson and staff, and on down the Road and to the Yankee line of Battle opposing Hood, the Yankees recived our advanced head of column with a Voley which seriously wounded Capt Crusman tore Genl Andersons feild glasses which were dangling by his side to peices and threw the whole of the Fourteenth Tenn Regt into such confusion that it took the officers sometime to straighten them out and form with the other Regiments a line of Battle. Which was something Genl Anderson didnt seem to know anything about. The men made the excuse for the General that his military experience in Mexico consisted of charging through the narrow streets of Towns "end foremost" and that he didnt know how to fight in the open country. At any rate Genl Anderson resigned within a few days and Col Robert Hatton of the 7th Tenn Regt was made Brigadier, and placed in command.[20] The enemy failing to interrupt Genl. Johnstons retreat the march was continued in the direction of Richmond and crossing the Chickahominy we went into camp almost in sight of the city. Where we lay awaiting the assembling of McClellands host until the opening of the Battle of Seven Pines May 31st 1862. In that Battle fell the Gallant General Robert Hatton, the Peer of any man in the Confederacy and with him many of the Brigade he commanded, and so gallantly led into action under the immediate eye of President Davis, Genl Lee,- and Johnston, the latter being severely wounded the command of the Army was placed in a short time in the able hands of Genl R.E. Lee Who proceeded at once to reorganize it into new Divisions, and Brigades.[21]

Col J. J. Archer of the Fourth Texas Regt was made a Brigadier, and placed in command of Hattons Brigade which was then composed of the 1st 7th and 14th Tenn Regts the 19th Georgia Regt and 5 Alabama Battalion the Brigade was attached to Genl A.P. Hills Division and took an active part in evry important engagement of the army of Northern Va. until Genl Hill was made Liut General after the Death of General Stonewall Jackson and placed in command of the 3d Corps of Army of Northern Va.-

A review of some of the more important service rendered by what was ever afterwards known as "Archer's Tennessee Brigade" as part of "A.P. Hills Light Division" will suffice to show the high position they held in the estimation of Generals Lee, Jackson, and Hill.

At the opening of "the Seven day Battles" around Richmond A.P. Hills were the first troops to cross the Chickahomany at Meadow Bridge and commence the assault on McClellands Right Flank at Mechanicsville, and then they led the advance at Gaines Mill with the Tennesseans in front to feel of an develop the Enemys position, in discharge of that duty the dead and wounded left on the borders of the old mill Race and in the Apple orchard where ordered to fall back; will attest as to how bravely they obeyed orders, and when they met other Brigades of the Division advancing to the charge promptly and as if on Parade took thier place on the left and soon joined to Hoods Brigade of Texans the Right of Jacksons Corps; and together they swept over the mill Race and two lines of Breast works and siezed the heights which were crowned with artilery that had swept the feild over which they had twice advanced.

The enemy fled in direst confusion leaving Artilery stores of all kinds with thier dead and wounded and many prisoners, thousands of small arms were thrown away, and camp equipage of all kinds left to be made use of. The result of this battle was the Tennessee Brigade no longer fought with the old smooth Bore musket with Buck & Ball but had the most improved Sprinfeild and Enfeild Rifles, and Braxtons Battery Artilery From Fredricksburg Va were given some of the splendid peices captured in place of thier old Guns they had handled so splendidly in the fight— this Battery had been attached to our Brigade and remained as a part of it until the organization of that Branch of the service into Batallions and all placed under the Cheif Artilery of the Army.

Other troops were put in front after the desperate work at "Gaines Mill" and the "Light Division was not called upon for any serious work until Fraziers Farm was reached, and the Tennessee Brigade was sent to the assistance of the Gallant South Carolinians under Genl R.H. Aderson [sic.] of Longstreets Division who was hotly engaged with Fitz John Porter. and we got there first in time to help to wrest from the enemy several peices of Artilery and drive them from the feild. The next day the Division was held in Reserve under the enemys heavy Artilery fire at "Malvern Hill" which was realy more trying than had been our active work in the front. McClelland having escaped to the protection of his Gun boats on the James River at Harrisons Landing, the "Light Division" was ordered back to Richmond.[22]

After a short stay there the Command was ordered to join Genl Stonewall Jackson near Gordonsville, and in the latter part of July 1862 the Light Division became a part of Jacksons 2nd Corps "Army of Northern Va" better known as the "foot cavalry." Soon afterwards Genl Jackson moved across the Rapidan to meet the advance of "Popes Army" under his old "commissary of the Valley"

"General Banks" and on Augst [sic.] 9th met and defeated the Federals at "Cedar Run" in a fiercely fought battle lasting from two oclock P.M. until after nightfall. The Division of Genl A.P. Hill with the Brigades of Archer and Pender in advance came on the feild about 4 P.M. just in time to meet and Drive back a heavy force of the enemy who had almost succeeded in turning the left of Earlys Division and were forceing our men back Brigadier Genl Winder Commanding the Stonewall Brigade had been mortally wounded and was being brought of the feild as Archers Brigade went into actoin [sic.] with the North Carolinians under Genl Pender on our left— we soon swept the feild captureing Brigadier Genl Prince, and most of his command.

The Tennessee Brigade lost quite heavily in thier charge across an open wheatfeild, among those who fell was Liut. Col. George Harrell of Fourteenth who was mortally wounded and afterwards died at Charlottsville Va.

After spending August 10th in burying our dead and removing the wounded Genl Jackson fell back across the Rapidan on the night of the 10th and we went in to camp near Orange Court House Where we were soon joined by "Longstreets corps" which had been left in front of Richmond to Watch McClelland movements.

"Pope" who had been placed in command of this new army by the Federal authorities at Washington Dubbed it in his Grandiloquent orders from "Headquarters in the Saddle" "the Grand Army of Virginia" and the Richmond Papers soon said that Lee and Jackson were making him keep his "Hindquarters in the saddle" trying to get back to Washington, and soon the man who boastingly had said he came from an Army in the West that had only seen the backs of thier enemies turned his back to Lee and placed the Rappahanock between him and the Confederate Army which had commenced the series of movements that resulted in his almost complete overthrow. On August 25th at sunrise Genl Jackson crossed the Rappahanock at Jeffersonton some miles above Warrenton Springs where Popes main force was assembled to prevent Genl Lee crossing the river; and with the men of his Corps unincumbered by knapsack or extra baggage moved silently around Popes Army and at Eleven oclock that night a portion of his forces bivuaced on the side of Thouroughfare Mountain more than 25 miles from thier starting Point of the morning. before Dawn of the 26th the silent column moved on through Thourghfare Gap, and before nightfall arrived at Bristow Station on the Orange and Alexandria R.R. Genl Jackson thus placing his Corps of Thirty Thousand men between Popes army of more than sixty Thousand and Washington City where McClellands Army from the James was being assembled to reinforce or cooperate with Pope. Great train loads of commisary, Quartermaster, and Ordinance stores were captured at Bristow and Mannassas junction where Archers Brigade spent the day of August 27th in resting feast Meanwhile from the many good things found in in the well filled sutlers stores and filling Haversacks with all they would hold, and that night the "Light Division" marched off by the light of the burning trains and warehouses containing many Thousands of Dollars worth of stores which we had no means of removing.

A.P. Hills Division moved across Bull Run, and took position on the 28th the Tennessee Brigade occupying a cut of an unfinished Rail Road and got ready for the coming of Popes army

Genl Ewels Division was engaged with the advance of Popes Army in the afternoon and that General lost a leg in the fight.

On the 29th Pope commenced the disposition of his forces to attack Jackson and in the afternoon made several attempts to dislodge Hills men from thier position in the R.R. cut but were repulsed with Great Slaughter, and when night came to our relief we calmly slept— feeling secure in our ability to repel all asaults from our foes as long as our ammunition Which was running low would hold out. in fact details from each company in the Fourteenth Regt. and probably others of Archers Brigade had been made to bring in the cartridges off the dead and wounded Federals in our front after they had been repulsed. and before the fighting ended on the 30th we were using thier own ammunition to a large extent to hold our position.

Longstreet having forced his way through Thouroughfare Gap which had been occupied by the Federals soon joined Jackson and assisted in repulsing the asaults of Popes forces on the afternoon of the 29th On the morning of the 30th all was quiet for a time but the seasoned veterans of Jacksons Corps felt in thier bones that it was the opening of the day that was to decide the issue between the two Armies. evry evidence of the concentration of a powerful force in Jacksons immediate front was indicated, and about Four oclock in the evening a furious attack was made upon Hills Division who still held thier Position in the "Rail Road Cut" three lines of Battle one after the other came and were successively repulsed with Great Slaughter; Genl Jackson then ordered his Whole line to charge thier broken lines and Longstreets men on the right joined in the irisistable onslaught and Popes "Grand Army of Virginia" was put to a disorganized and disgraceful flight— which was continued to the friendly works crowning the heights of Centreville In this last change Col. W.A. Forbes of the Fourteenth Tenn Regt fell mortally wounded with many others of the Regt- and Brigade.[23]

Genl Jacksons Corps was ordered on towards Washington and on Sept 1st late in the evening came on the enemy in position at Ox Hill or Germantown and immediately attacked them in the midts of a terific rain storm; after a short engagement the enemy hastily retreated leaving two of thier General officers Phil Kearney and Stevens dead on the feild.

The Corps was then ordered to Leesburg Va and on Sept 5th Passed the Potomac at Whites Ford and entered Maryland to feast at supper on Green corn cooked by fires made by the rails that surrounded the feild in which the corn grew.

The next day we occupied Fredrick, and remained there until the 10th of Sept and then proceeded to Williamsport forded the river; reentered Va and proceeded at once to Martinsburg the garison of Federals fled to Harpers Ferry at the approach of Genl Jackson who at once followed them we reached Harpers Ferry on the 13th that day and the 14th of Sept was spent in getting into communication with Genl McLaws on Maryland Heights and Genl Walker on Louden Heights overlooking the Town and and to some extent the enemys fortification on Bolivar Heights to the Southwest , and along this range of Highlands the Federals had thier Main line of Defensive works and they were manned with 70 pieces of Artilery and garrison of Eleven thousand Infantry. Hills Division on the right was to storm the the [sic] enemys main works immediately after a cessation of the fire of Artilery and Archer's Brigade was just ready to move on the main Fort when the white Flag appeared and soon Archers Brigade marched into the works Genl A.P. Hill leading and more than Eleven Thousand Federals surrendering With 73 peices of Artilerery [sic.] and vast quantities of stores of All kinds. Genl Jackson left Genl Hill to recive the Surrender and Parole the prisoners and remove the captured arms and stores while he with the other forces hastened to the aid of Genl. Lee who was engaged with McLellands vast army at Sharpsburg Md. The 16th was spent by the Fourteenth on duty in one of the large buildings where were stored vast quantities of Quartermaster supplies, ostensibly as a guard, but realy in appropriating whatever might suit the fancy of any one individual to his own personal use. Orders were recieved on the night of the 16th to be ready to move at an early hour on the 17th and at sun rise "Archers Brigade" crossed Bolaver Heights and but for the tattered Battle flags might have been taken for a brand new Brigade from Boston so completely were they clothed in Yankee uniforms. The line of march was at once taken in the direction of Sharpsburg, the omnious [sic] roar of cannon telling the men of the old Light Division that comrades under Lee, Longstreet, and Jackson were engaged in a mighty strugle with McLellands Hosts. and with quick step they moved out on that forced march of Eighteen miles. an occasional stop of a few minutes for rest left the place marked by many cast off blue garments and the old faded Gray coat or jacket took the place of the blue Blouse or [illegible] an officers fine coat.

Wading the Potomac at Botelers ford and hurrying on the heights over looking the Anteitam Valley was reached and the bursting shells with voleys of musketry accompanied by the "Hip, Hip Hurrah" of the Yankees told us that our men were being forced back. With the unerring instinct of the true soldier Genl Hill took in the situation realizing that the Right flank of Lees Army was being turned by Burnsides overwhelming force they already having gotten possession of the Road to Shepperdstown, with lightning rapidity the Division was formed in line at first sweeping back the enemy who had reached the "Road" and almost at the sametime [sic] recapturing a Battery that had fallen into thier hands. the Light Division charged across an open feild of fresh plowed land at the father side of which we came in sight of a "stone fence" behind which was a strong force of the enemy wich was reinforced before we could reach it by another strong line but the Light Division went on and Drove the enemy from the fence and back to the banks of the Anteitam Creek under cover of thier Artilery advantageously posted on the other side. Thus A.P. Hill with his skeleton Division of not exceeding Three Thousand effective men after a forced march of 18 miles entered the fight at 4 P.M. and drove Burnsides Fifteen

Thousand from the feild and held it until the night of the 19th when Genl Lee withdrew his army across the Potomac leaving only his wounded that could not be moved.[24]

Archer's Brigade waded the Potomac on the early morning of the 20th of Sept and moved three of [sic] four miles in the direction of Martinsburg Va. and went into camp but in a short time was ordered back in the direction of the Potomac when we found a force of the enemy in position on the southside of the River the Brigades of Pender and Archer were soon formed and in a short time advanced upon the federals who were formed in line parallel with the river a position of them occupying a high Bluff. the Fourteenth Tenn Regt came in contact with that part of the federal line in the ensuing charge and drove them over the Bluff or captured many of them the route of the whole force was as complete as could be. remaining on the feild until after nightfall the command moved back to camp

After a short time we were ordered to Bunker Hill between Winchester and Harpers ferry. where the Regiment with other troops of the Division enjoyed a much needed rest and where our Ranks was much strengthened by many sick, wounded, and footsore men who had been compelled to forego the hardships of the strenuous campaign from Cedar Run to Shepperdstown, a portion of the time was spent by the 2nd corps in tearing up the Baltimore & Ohio R.R. the most direct line from Washington to the West. that work and a slight demonstration by the Federals coming through Snickers Gap to Castlemans Ferry on the Shenandoah River which Archer and one other Brigade Repulsed on Nov 6th was all that interfered with our enjoyment of this period of rest and recuperation.

About this time McClelland was removed from command of the federal army and Burnside placed in command. and soon commenced to concentrate his army opposite Fredricksburg on the Rappahanock River. and Genl Jackson was ordered to join

Genl Lee at that place, and commenced his march across the Blue ridge from Winchester on Nov 22nd reaching the vicinity of Fredricksburg on Dec 1st and going into camp near Guineas Station where we remained in camp until ordered to take our place in the front line of Jacksons Corps just to the left of Hamiltons Crossing and the "Light Division" held the front line of Jacksons Corps along the foot of the hills that terminate in the cleared level lands of the River bottom more than a mile wide and across which the Federal left wing had to advance to reach our line.

A heavy fog which covered the whole plain on the morning of Dec 13th about Eleven oclock the mist rolled away and revealed one of the most imposing sights ever beheld on the American continent. Marshalled in front of Jacksons Corps was the two Corps of Hooker and Franklin estimated at Fifty Five Thousand men formed in three lines of battle. And after a preliminary Artillery Duel they commenced to advance across that wide plain. When they had reached within 800 yards of our line our artilery near Hamiltons opened up and other Batteries joined and complled them to retire to the shelter of a Road near the river and remained passive until shortly after noon. Then they advanced with three lines of Battle again, coming on in front of "Archer" until they reached the Rail Road some 75 yards in our front and then Archer gave the word "Fire" and a storm of lead was poured upon those in our front that caused them to melt away as did the mist of the morning before the sun. A force through to our left penetrated a peice of woods occupied by Lanes Brigade, and forcing them back came around the left and rear of Archer, and before we were aware of what had occurred they were shooting our men in their backs several of the Fourteenth was shot and a number of the Brigade was captured soon however Genl Archer reformed his Brigade and with the assistance of Lawtons Georgia Brigade drove them out of the woods killing and capturing many of them. Thus ended one of the most sanguinary Battles of the war for the federals. and our loss would not have been noticeble but for the incursion made by the force that overcame Lane in the woods to our left. Col Peter Turney of the First Tenn Regt was severely wounded in this Battle.

The Enemy being disastrously replulsed also by Longstreets

forces who held Mayres Hill on the Left soon gave up any further effort to dislodge Genl Lee and withdrew thier entire army to the North side of the Rappahannock and soon both armies Went into Winter quarters. Archers Brigade was given a place near Guineas Station. and soon had comfortable cabins, or good chimneys to their Tents.

In January of 1863 a detail was made by order of the War Department of one man from each company in the Three Tennessee Regts. to go to Tennessee and get recruits for thier respective commands.[25] As the Federals had possession of most of the territory from which the Fourteenth Regiment had been raised, and had held it since the fall of Fort Donelson the undertaking was fruitless; as those who would enlist at all preferred to join some command in Bragg's army opperating nearer thier homes and most of those who were not in the regular service already were connected with some Band of independent Bushwackers or Guerillas who put in thier time mostly in dodging Yankee Scouting parties or in stealing from the defenceless women and children the little they had left to live on. Many of these were the families of men at the Front in Braggs or Lees army.

After a long rest in winter quarters the last days of April found Jacksons Corps actively engaged in preparations to meet the advance of Hooker who had succeeded Burnside in command of the Federals. On the 29th of April Sedgwick Commanding the left of Hookers Army Crossed the river and took position in front of Jackson at Hamiltons crossing and made feint of attack meantime Hooker was moveing up the Rappahannock with the main body of his army with the purpose of crossing the Rappidan River and placing his army on the left and Rear of Genl Lee, and thus compel him to give up his strong possition at Fredricksburg. On April the 30th Genl Jackson leaving Genl Early with his division to watch Sedgwick, hastened with the ballance of the Corps to Genl Lees assistance who was watching Hooker in his strongly fortified position at Chancellorsville. After defeating Hookers efforts to open communication with Sedgwick by way of Banks Ford on May 2nd and Hooker having gone back to his fortified position around Chancolorsville, Genls Lee and Jackson met in consultation as to how and where to attack Hooker on the morning of May

2nd and there seated on a log "Near the Plank Road" there was formed the plan of the Great Movement to be executed by Genl Jackson and Corps. Alas for our Cause the last to be conducted by that Great Soldier, but the one that placed the Crown of Military genious on his brow and will forever proclaim him as one of the greatest of Warriors; at Sunrise on the morning of May 2nd Genl Lee stood on the roadside to see Jacksons troops file by for the great flank movement was begun; and soon Genl Jackson himself came riding along and Jackson halted for a few minutes and had a short conversation with Gen Lee. And then he rode on with his column who in silence moved with quick step each man seemed to feel that they were bent on some great mission, and while in ignorance as to its aim or object, perfect confidence in the great soldier leading them was such as to leave no doubt in thier minds as to the outcome:

Thus was the boastful Hooker fooled as he lay in his fortified position with Lee confronting his great army of ninety Thousand men with not more than Fifteen Thousand. While Jackson with Twenty six Thousand sought his right flank and rear. After a march of twelve or fifteen miles at 2 oclock Genl Fitz Lee commanding the Cavalry that moved with Jackson discovered that our force had reached a point favorable for attack upon the Right and rear of Hookers line held by Howards Corps; The troops of Jackson were formed in line of battle Rodes Division in front, Colston next and A.P. Hills division in the third line[26]

About 6 PM all being ready Genl Jackson ordered the advance. And with a cheer the men of his corps burst upon the unsuspecting foe—capturing cannon and hundreds of men. And almost anilating Howards Corps, and doubling Sickles Corps back on Hookers left near Chancellorsville. Darkness brought the victorious advance of Jackson to a temporary halt, and his lines were being reformed Genl A.P. Hills division placed in front with orders to continue the pursuit, and soon after the lamentable shooting of Genl Jackson by our own men occured which with the wounding of Genl Hill put a stop to any further advance that night. And Genl Stuart was placed in command of Jacksons corps. At early dawn on the 3d pressed the Corps forward Hills division in the front line Trimbles in second and Rodes in rear, and at 8 am stormed the enemy works which after a desperate struggle led by

Stuart in person was carried and held. At this point Archers Brigade executed a move which resulted in the capture of a Federal Battery that gave our artilery a very commanding position of the feild stil held by the federals. And which was soon occupied by Maj Pegram with his Battalion of artilery, in speaking of this movement afterwards Genl A.P. Hill said "Archers Brigade were the Heroes of Chancellorsville". for the position gained made the compelling of Hooker to finally yeild his position at easy Chancellorsville.[27] Wich was at 10 Am won, with assistance of Anderson & McLaws divisions. Hooker withdrew to a strong position near the Rappahanock and in a driving rainstorm he withdrew his badly beaten army across the river that night

A.P. Hills Division moved back to thier old position to the right of Fredricksburg and remained there until ordered to follow Genl Lee who with Longstreet and Ewells Corps were already in the Shanndoah Valley. Jacksons Corps was divided and formed the 2nd corps under Genl Ewell, and the 3d corps under Liut Genl A.P.Hill wich was composed of the Divisions of Gen Pender Genl Anderson and Genl H. Heth to the latter division "Archers Brigade" was attached; Genl Lee with Ewells forces captured Winchester with Four Thousand Prisoners twenty odd peices of Artilery, wagons, Horses, and immense supply of stores and amunition. On the 24th of June the whole of Genl Lees Army was across the Potomac, in magnificent fighting trim, and ready to meet and try conclusion with the enemy on thier own soil.

"Hills Corps" camped at Cashtown Pa. And from there on the morning of July 1st commenced the march to Gettysburg five miles distant. And at the time held by "Bufords division of Federal Cavalry" with thier advanced line of skirmishers well out on the Cashtown Pike. "Archers Brigade" led the advance of "Heths division" the head of A.P. Hills column and soon came in contact with Bufords dismounted men whom they hurriedly forced back towards Gettysburg; and by ten oclock Am we came in sight of the Town and were pushing Bufords men back into the "Seminary" Grove when a federal Battery dashed out and took position on the Ridge and opened fire on Archers advancing line whos rapid pursuit of "Buford" had seperated him from the other Brigades of Heth who were a mile or more behind; when the Battery opened on Archers men they raised a yell and charged across Willoughby

Run; and into the Seminary Grove and there met the advance of Reynolds corps composed of Indianians and known as the "Iron Brigade" Archers advance was checked; and soon the enemy in great force appeared on his Right flank & rear and compelled a hasty withdrawal of all the lines to the Left. Genl Archer with about two hundred of his men were captured and the Brigade fell back until they met the other Brigades of Heth a mile from the scene of our morning fight Col B.D. Fry of the 13th Ala Regt took command of the Brigade and we took part in the movements that led to the capture of the Town later in the day; and which we could have done much easier in the morning if the troops in our rear had kept up with the advance of Archer and given him the proper support as it was the Brigade inflicted a heavy loss on the enemy, especially in the death of Genl Reynolds one of thier best officers. To the men of the old Brigade the capture of Genl Archer caused great regret. On the night of the first, Hills Corps was placed to the right of the Town and spent July 2nd in rear of the forces in front of Cemetery Hill and ridge, and took no part in in [sic.] the fighting of that day.

On the morning of July 3d Hills Corps moved to the right and took position to the left of Longstreets corps, Archers Brigade was joined to the left of Picketts Division and the other Brigades of Heths division extended the line to the left which was further extended by Lanes and Scales Brigades of Penders division under command of Genl Trimble. The line thus formed constituted the Assaulting column, and the orders were to "dress on the centre" And "Archers Brigade" held the centre At one oclock a signal Gun broke the stillness then another signal Gun, and then all along Seminary Ridge the flame from more than one hundred cannon burst forth, and with Iron hail swept the Federal position on Cemetery Ridge; "gun answerd gun, and for two hours the two armies were wrapt in the smoke of the most tremendous cannonade that ever in the open feild darkened the sky of the western world."

At the end of two hours the fire ceased and Lees line arose from the ground and "dressed to the centre" Col. B.D. Fry of the 13th Alabama better known as ("old Nicauraga") commanded Archers Brigade." The confederate infantry clad in sombre homespun with nothing bright about them but thier bloodied Battle flags and the glittering sheen of cold steel," moved out to that death charge as if on Parade, under the eye of thier great commander Genl Lee. Soon the cannon of the enemy opened sending shot and shell through the advancing lines, makeing wide gaps that was almost as soon closed by the sturdy veterans. The waving battle flags seemed to be the special mark as soon as we came in range of the small arms. Three men being shot with the colors of the Fourteenth Tenn Regt before the "Crest" at the Stone fence was reached. The names of those three men deserve to appear in letters in Gold in the most conspicuous place in the State House at Nashville They were Thomas Davidson,[28] Color bearer (Co G), Columbus Horn,[29] Color Corporal (co G) and — Powell— (Co C) Color Corporal, who fell apparently dead just after crossing the Emmetsburg Pike, and within one hundred yards of the stone fence from there it was carried by Barney Smith of (Co F) to the stone fence from which the Enemy fled, and at which place it was captured by the federals when they retook thier lines, from which we had to flee before overpowering numbers. Archers Brigade lost three fourths of thier number, few of the companies had a commission officer left Col. Fry was severely wounded and most all the feild officers of the different Regts of the Brigade were killed or wounded.[30] When those that escaped reached our Artillery they found Genl Lee and others rallying the stragling few that got back just in rear of Pegrams Battalion of Artilery, whos men was standing by thier Guns in readiness to repel any advance of the enemy, but it seemed they were not anxious to try conclusions with us again after thier experience of the day.

The brigade Bivuaced near the Ground occupied before the charge was made; and remained there unmolested all day of July 4th, and early in the night of the 4th commenced our retreat to Haggerstown Md by way of the Fairfeild Pike marching all night in a drizling rain; and reached Hagerstown Md the next day where Genl Lee halted and fortified a strong position, the Federal Army under Mead "soon came up and took position in front of our works, but that wary General made no attack, and a little desultory fireing between the Skirmishers of the two armies was all that took place during the several days they confronted each other at Hagerstown.

On the night of July 13th Genl Lees army commenced falling back to the Potomac river in the midts of of a driveing rain Storm which made the roads almost impassible—Heths Division again had the "place of honor" as rear Guard of Lees Army and after an all nights march of a few miles through slush and mud reached a point about a mile from Falling Water, where the Army was crossing the river on a Pontoon; we were halted and formed in line facing towards Hagerstown, the Tennessee Regts being immediately to the left of the Road leading back to Hagerstown some light earthworks built by some of the troops that preceeded us in form of Rifle Pits, were occupied by the 14th Tenn Regt—and we were permitted to take a much needed rest— many of the men throwing themselves on the wet ground were soon lost to all sense of care or danger, as we had been informed that a body of our Cavalry was between us and the enemy, and were cautioned not to fire on them when they approached.

About Eleven oclock A.m. the Sleepers were aroused by the cry that the "Yankee Cavalry" was coming, and sure enough there was a body of them coming in column of fours with thier sabres drawn and the Stars and Stripes floating over them. Some of the men commenced to shoot and the officers tried to restrain them, but at the first crack of our rifles the advancing horsemen were ordered to charge, and in a few minutes they were right in our midst cutting and shooting and for a short time there was a hand to hand strugle between this battalion of drunken cavalry and a remnant of Lees veteran infantry it did not last long; for when one of our rifles fired a man or horse one fell; we being at such close quarters that it was almost impossible to miss; the officers for once had a good opportunity to use thier side arms with telling effect, it was said that Capt Norris of the 7th Tenn Regt brought down three with his Colts Navy at Short range. At any rate of the more than two hundred Michigan Cavalry who composed this squadron which proved to be the advance Guard of Kilpatricks Corps, only a few were left to tell the tale.[31] But the canteens of most of those left on the feild told the tale as to why they were so desperatly brave; and foolhardy. Only a few minutes elapsed before the large feilds to our right and front was covered with Kilpatricks cavalry and they were already closing in on the right of our line where they captured some of Heths Division. When the orders were given for each man to make his way to trhe River as best they could, and then a wild race commenced to reach the Pontoon Bridge. Most of "Archers Brigade" made thier wasy through a body of woods through which run a small stream and by following the General directions of this Branch we soon reached the Tow Path of the Chesapeake and Ohio Canal which run along side of the river and we were none too soon in reaching this point for when we looked up the "Tow Path" the head of a column of Federal infantry were in sight marching in column of fours, and one impudent fellow some hundred yards in advance ordered a squad of us to surrender we called him to us as if hesitating and when he came up notwithstanding his assurance that "the war was over" we took him in tow on the "Tow Path", and made double quick time for the Bridge a short distance below, and we could hear the resounding footbeats of our comrades as they hurried over and our own movements were quickeneed, when coming in sight of the Bridge we beheld the men with uplifted axes ready to cut the ropes and let it swing around to the sout side of the river. And more than one pleading voice was heard to call out "Dont cut that rope there is lots of our men over here yet." "The Tow path" prisoner was carried to Genl Lee, and he was informed of the approach of the enemy on the Tow Path when he ordered a battery to throw a few shells across the river, which checked thier advance on the Bridge, and in a short time the ropes was Cut and it swung around leaving quite a number of our men to fall into the hands of the enemy.

The wearied men glad once more to be on Virginia soil, and for the time free from molestation from Mead and his men, bivuacked near the river, and found a good nights rest. Shoes were issued to many who had been doing strenuous duty on the march, in the trenches at Haggerstown, and at Falling Water with bare, and sore feet since leaving Gettysburg.

On the 15th the army moved in the directoin [sic] of Winchester and from thier to Culpepper "Archers Brigade" held the post of honor as rear guard and from time to time, were engaged in repelling attacks of Federal Cavalry under "Genl Custer" who made himself and command exceedingly conspicuous in trying to interfere with the movements of our wagon Trains. We were successful in repelling them; not without some sharp fighting at times, but mostly with considerable loss to them.

"Archers Brigade" having been greatly reduced in numbers with many companies not having a commissioned officerto command and our feild officers killed or captured was now for the time consolidated with Brockenbroughs Virginia Brigade under Brigadier Genl H.H. Walker and remained under his command until he was severely wounded on May 6th 1864 while holding the right Flank of Lees Army againts [sic.] Grant in the Wilderness.

The mortally wounding of Brigadier Genl Pettigrew by the Yankee Cavalry in the fight at Falling Water should have been mentioned, as he was in immediate command of the rear Guard of the army, and was one of the finest soldiers and most efficient officiers Genl Lee had.

After crossing the Rappahanock and resting a few days Genl Lee took position on the south of the Rapidan River, and Archers Brigade went to camp near Orange CourtHouse where the time was spent in visiting and drilling; with the exception of the flank movement by which Genl Lee Compelled "Meade" to fall back to Centreville early in October, and the unfortunate affair at Bristoe Station. Nothing of importance occured till on Nov 26th nearly 5 months after "Meades" so called great victory over Genl Lees forces at Gettysburg; the Federal army crossed the Rapidan and after finding Genl Lees army posted behind "Mine Run" and ready to recive an attack, but Meade knew better than to attack Lees army behind breastworks, and on the night of Dec 1st withdrew his army to the North side of the Rapidan and we were back to our winter quarters near Orange C.H. and the 14th Tenn Regt passed the time in Picket duty on the Rapidan, and Drilling, until the 14th of Dec the Regiment recieved orders to be ready to move immediately and cooked Rations went to the Railroad at Orange C.H. boarding a train and went in direction of Gordonsville and thence to Staunton, and was immediately ordered Buffalo Gap and went into Bivuack on the Monterey Pike, as a force of the enemys cavalry was reported to be advancing on Staunton. The Regiment was entirely without Tents and the weather was extremely cold and on the night of Dec 16th about ten oclock it commenced to rain & sleet, and continued until next day. On Thursday 17th Dec at 1 PM we were ordered to Staunton and found shelter in houses and barns as best we could for the night;

on the 19th we moved through Staunton in direction of Harrisonburg, camped at Mount Craawford, and marched a [sic] 5 am drove the Yankee Pickets down the Valley, and on the 22nd moved to Mount Jackson where we went into camp and remained there until after New Year, 1864, and fared well with the Good people of the Valley. Genl Imbodens Cavalry being between us and the enemy we had no extra hard duty to perform.[32]

In January 1864 the Regt was ordered back in direction of Harrisonburg and went into camp near "Cross Keys" where the greater part of the time was spent until the Regiment was ordered back to the army near Orange C.H. in March 1864. Col. Wm McComb was in command of the 14th having returned after several months abscence on account of wounds.[33] After the return of the 14th Regt to the army, the time was spent in drilling or Picket duty until the opening of the campaign on May 4th when orders came to cook rations and be ready to move at a moments notice. And Heths Division moved out towards Chancellorsville and Bivuaced at Mine Run that night; and early on the morning of May 5th the division resumed its march and soon met the enemys skirmishers on the Plank Road consisting of dismounted cavalry— "reaching a point on the Plank road about a half a mile west of where it crosses the Brock road at right angles, at which the enemy refused to be driven any further. "At this Point Genl Heth deployed his division as it came up" in line of battle,— at 4 Pm Hancock and Getty made an attack on Heths Line and were reinforced by the divisions of Birney and Mott. as the fight progressed, and before the Close by four other Brigades

It will be well to give here the account of this terrific Battle in the words of "Private Leigh Robinson in an address before the Army of Northern Virginia Association at Richmond on the first of November 1877."[34] "Comrade Robinson who was a participant, says: "About half past three oclock or a little latter Lee had sent an officer of his staff (Col Marshall) to Heth with this message: "General Lee directs me to say that it is very important for him to have possession of the Brock Road and wishes you to take that position if you can without bringing on a general engagement." Heth replied in effect, that the only way to find out whether it would or would not bring on a general engagement, was to make the attempt to take the position, which he would make if desired.

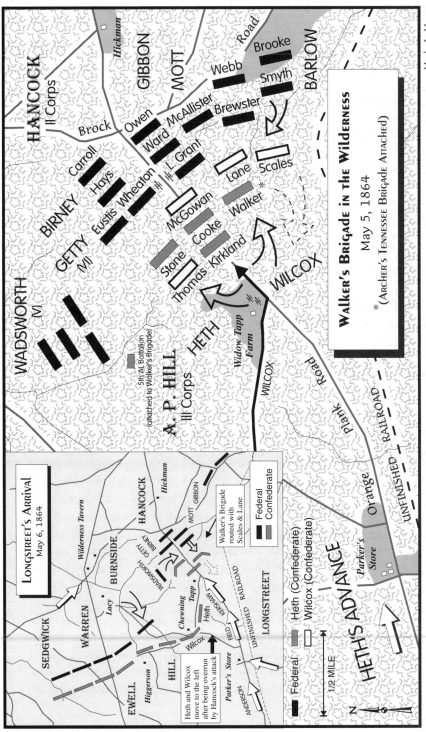

Mark A. Moore

Walker's Brigade in the Wilderness

May 5, 1864

*(Archer's Tennessee Brigade Attached)

HANCOCK
II Corps

GIBBON

MOTT

BARLOW

Brooke

Webb

Smyth

Hickman

Brock

Owen

Ward

McAllister

Brewster

Carroll

Hays

L. Grant

Lane

Scales

BIRNEY

Eustis

Wheaton

McGowan

Walker

GETTY
(VI)

Stone

Cooke

Thomas

Kirkland

WILCOX

WADSWORTH
(V)

5th AL Battalion
(attached to Walker's Brigade)

A. P. HILL
III Corps

HETH

Widow Tapp
Farm

WILCOX

Plank
Road

Road

UNFINISHED
RAILROAD

Orange

Parker's
Store

HETH'S ADVANCE

Longstreet's Arrival
May 6, 1864

Wilderness Tavern

Hickman

HANCOCK

GIBBON
MOTT

Walker's Brigade
routed with
Scales & Lane

Federal
Confederate

SEDGWICK

WARREN

BURNSIDE

GETTY
BIRNEY

WADSWORTH

Lacy

Chewning

Tapp

Heth

Higgerson

HILL

EWELL

Parker's
Store

Heth and Wilcox
move to the left
after being overrun
by Hancock's attack.

KIRSHAM

FIELD

UNFINISHED
RAILROAD

ANDERSON

LONGSTREET

Federal
Heth (Confederate)
Wilcox (Confederate)

1/2 MILE

N

Before a reply could be recieved he was himself attacked with great fury. We had not thrown up the usual impromptu breastworks; we were in a body of woods, studded thick with heavy undergrowth. The enemy was for time fully disclosed, when within about ninety yards. He was driven back, so soon as the first attacking columns could be cleared away a second column advanced to share the fate of the first. A third a fourth a fifth advanced. These assaults were well prepared and well delivered They were not victorious", but no one can say they were ineffectual. The equal fierceness of brave men was locked in those lonely shadows. The issue had come to this simple one: Who can stand the most killing?

On one side of such issue, Heth with not quite seven thousand muskets, held at bay for nearly two hours, Hancock and Getty; Hancock alone having Twenty seven thousand muskets and supporting the attack with his Whole corps. I say Heth; it should be Heth and his brigade commanders and the men they commanded—all welded into one feirce sword, whos handle rested in Heths grasp. And whos temper it may well be his pride to have matched with his own. The brigade commanders were Colonel J.M. Stone, Brigadier General John R. Cooke, Brigadier General H.H. Walker, and Brigadier General W.W. Kirkland. The names of the men they commanded I cannot give you."

This splendid tribute to the gallant Harry Heth and the men he commanded in this most unequal struggle by comrade "Robinson" has been given place in these memoirs because "Archers Brigade of Tennesseans were there under the command of Brigadier Genl H.H. Walker, and held the extreme right of Genl Lees Army, where some of the hardest of the fighting was done in order to repel the repeated efforts of Hancock to turn our right flank and get possession of the Plank Road and compell the withdrawal of the forces in his immediate front that he had failed to move by direct assault.[35] Night brought to an end this terific struggle and left Heth and Wilcox, in full possession of the feild, early in the night Heths Division was moved back a short distance to the rear and the different Regiments, and Brigades became intermingled in the darkness the word was given out in someway that Hills Corps would be relieved by Longstreets corps by three oclock in the morning and that Hill would Move to the right. All through the night the enemy could be heard felling trees and fortifying in front of our position of the evening before, and the men of Heth and Wilcoxs division kept ask each other why they were not allowed to build breastworks too.

And so the night wore on, three oclock came, then four and no word of Longstreet or sign of his coming. And those seasoned veterans of Heth and Wilcox as if by intuition warned of impending danger commenced to arouse themselves; and as the first streaks of early dawn appeared in the east could be seen hurriedly rolling up thier blankets and oil clothes, and without orders making evry preperation for a hasty move. When all at once the mechanical "Whoop Hurah Hurah" of the Yankees accompanied by a volley of musketry caused evry man to spring to thier feet and grasp thier guns, the different regiments mixed as they were without semblance of order or alighnment, with a solid line of federals in veiw [sic]; did what was perfectly natural under the circumstances, someone has said, "Genl Heth had ordered his brigade commanders to take thier men to the rear as fast as possible, in effect the men were ordered to run", Be that as it may evry mothers son of them was soon running at topmost speed. "And "if they did not severally" show a clean pair of heels, it was because the same was not there to be shown". It did not take long for this fleeing host to meet the advance of Longstreets men Hoods Texas Brigade the Texans and Tennesseans had been together in Whitings division in the pennsul campaign under Genl J.E. Johnston, and there were many of the Texans who had gone to Texas from middle Tennessee before the war and consequently many acquaintances were formed or renewed by men of the two Brigades, and there existed a mutual high regard for each other among the men of the two commands, and right there occurred something unusual and out of the ordinary. The Tennesseeans being at the time consolidated with Walkers Virginia brigade, and under the command of Genl H.H. Walker since the capture of Genl Archer and the wounding of Col Fry at Gettysburg,— the Tennesseeans on all occassions when asked to what command they belonged, took especial pains to say "Archers Tennessee Brigade"

But when the Gallant Texans opened ranks to let the flying fugitives pass through to at least present safety and asked "What command is this" "Walkers Virginia Brigade" the ledgend says was the unvaried reply, until one of the Texans recognized a member of Fourteenth Tenn Regt—who had proclaimed in tones not be be misunderstood that it was "Walkers Virginia Brigade" and the Texan replied in stentorian tone "the Hell when did you fellows get a transfer from "Archers Tennessee Brigade" and ever after that the Texans would say the Tennesseans as they passed each other by saying there goes "Walkers Virginia Brigade" "didnt they run through at the Wilderness"

But be it to the credit of the men who held the feild against the hosts of Hancock and Getty on the day before within a half an hour aftern passing through Longstreets lines to the rear, they had rallied and returned to the front and with no sign of demoralization took thier places ready to go as far or stay as long, as the Gallant Texans which was all that men could do.[36]

More has been written here than otherwise would, but for the prominent part taken by the Tennesseans in the battle of the 5th to be followed by the unfortunate occurrence which caused the retreat on the morning of the 6th of May. One thing though is well known. It was not the fault of the rank and file of Heths division for even a proper alignment in the open woods without breastworks; would have prevented a successful advance of the enemy, and with the breastworks which the men were eager to build during the night, Grants whole army could not have moved Heth and Wilcoxs divisions by a front attack. And another thing is well known: that is nowhere recorded in History that either Stonewall Jackson, Ewell, or A.P. Hill ever failed to be at a certain place at a certain time when ordered by Genl Lee for he did not expect or ask his subordinates to do the impossible. It is true Longstreet was late getting there, but he and his men did heroic work after they did arrive if the night had been two hours longer, or they had come even an hour sooner how different might have been the results of that days fighting. With Hills Corps lapping around Grants left flank and Longstreet driving his front as he did do until shot by his own men, it would have been another such inglorious feild as that of nearby Chancellorsville is the belief of those who took part in the fighting of May the fifth.

Longstreets fall and Ewells partial success on the right of Grants army brought to a close the opperations in the Wilderness and Grant commenced his movement to the right of Lee that landed his Grant army at Spotsylvania Court House. Where he again found Genl Lee across his path and again ready to give him battle, Heths division took position almost in front of the Town and at once went to work to build breastworks the Tennesseans were just to the left of the Court House and the Fourteenth Tenn Regt was placed just to the left of where the works made a sharp angle and bore away to the left a few hours found not only Heths division behind formidable works but Lees whole army, and when Grant commenced on the 9th and 10th of May to feel our front he discovered that we had learned to protect ourselves, and that it would be no childs play to even try to take those works; on the 10th Warrens federal corps tried to turn our extreme left. But was driven back across the Mataponi in confusion by Hills Corps under command of Genl Early, Genl Hill being sick. the Tennesseans were in the fight to the finish, and we moved back to our breastworks that night, and remained there until Grant gave up trying to force Lees front and again moved to Lees right after spending several days in "manuevering," a thing he at one time said he "never did".[37]

On the 20th of May he again moved by his left flank and crossed the North Anna River, and here the Tennesseeans made one of the best fights they ever made under the Command of Col. Wm. McComb of the Fourteenth Regt.[38]

Grant failing in his effort at North Anna, withdrew his forces and commenced the mannueverring tactics again which landed his grand army at Cold Harbor where he found Genl Lee ready to meet him with his heroic veterans sheltered behind formidable Breast works the constructions of which they had become perfect adepts in. Genl Grant having ordered up sixteen thousand of Butlers men from South of the James" on June the 3d at break of day assaulted Lees entire front resolved to break through the Slender barrier that opposed his advance on Richmond but when the smoke of conflict cleared, the barrier was still there, but Grants army was a wreck and thier own historians says they "sullenly refused to obey orders, and again advance."[39]

Grant now decided to move his army across James River and approach Richmond from the South "seize Petersburg by a coup De Main", But his plans failed and when his Army reached the works of Petersburg they found the veterans of Lee filling them and ready to repeat the terrible work of the Wilderness Spotsylvania and Cold Harbor. On June the 18th Hills Corps reached Petersburg and took thier places in the line of works already practically constructed and which they at once proceeded to make as strong and complete as any earthworks ever constructed on the american continent, fighting by day and building Breast works at night was carried on regularly by the men of Heths division for weeks the service being the most arduous of any in the experience of the Tennesseans along that line, during the War. However it is not be understood that Genl Lee intended to confine his army to a mere defenscive force behind breastwork; neither did he do it, but repeatedly ventured forth and administered stinging blows to his adversary, for when Grant tried to extend his left so as to get possession the Weldon Rail Road on June 22nd Mahone with three Brigades and in a terrific fight at the "Johnson House" whiped Birneys, Motts, and Gibbons divisions and returned to the lines with more than seventeen Hundred prisoners four peices of artilery and eight stand of colors. Then come the battle of the Crater and while the Tennesseans being at the time north of the James were not in the fight they made one of the hardest marches of more than twenty miles from Sunrise until twelve oclock in order to reach Petersburg a help thier hard pressed comrades who we found had completely foild the enemy and had inflicted great loss upon them.

Then came the battles of August 18th fought by Heths division, and the 19th when Heth and Mahone captured many standards and more than twenty seven hundred prisoners. in all these fights the Tennesseeans took part and also on August 25th in the battle of Reams Station, then came the battles of the "Jones House" on September 30th and October 1st in which many prisoners were captured. After this a period of comparative quiet reigned until Oct 27th the Battle of "Hatchers Run" was fought in all these Battles the Brigade was commanded by Genl Wm McComb former colonel of the Fourteenth Tenn Regiment Genl Archer having died soon after being Exchanged.

Then came the trials of that long and dreary last winter of the war when the men of Lees army lived on one sixth of a ration of corn meal and rancid pork—The trials and sufferings of that winter is known to and can only be fully realized by those who endured them.[40] With the men ten paces a part in the Trenches often; and not more than an interval of twenty four hours between duty on picket or in the trenches the men were worn to to [sic] the point where physical ability in many instances to perform the duty was almost impossible.[41]

And then matters went on until Gordons assault on Grants right which failed because of not being supported as expected on March 25 1865 and the disaster that came at Five Forks on Apl 1st and then on the morning of April 2nd Grants Hosts broke the thin grey line to the right of Petersburg. And it fell to the lot of the Tennesseeans under Genl Wm McComb to make the last attempt to retake the broken line, And to thier credit be it said that they went at the work with the same spirit that animated them on scores of other feilds, and in that last grand effort of this little Brigade the lives of some of the bravest and best were sacrificed in the endeavor to accomplish the impossible.[42] Notably Capt Harry Bullock of (Co G) 14th Tenn Reg. Bob Keesee of (Co B), and many others of the Regiment killed or wounded, others will tell of what occurred in other Regiments finally when driven back towards Hatchers Run by overwhelming numbers, the order was given for evry man to make his way out as best they could and to assemble at Amelia Court House. Many were captured and a small disorganized remnat succeeded in crossing the Appomatox River and reached the main body of the army at Amelia Court House, and followed on to Appomatox Court House, where the "curtain fell"; and what had been the greatest Army in point of valor and grand achievements passed out of existence; with no stain of dishonor upon them they furled thier Battle flags; and turned thier faces towards thier desolated homes, to commence life anew, and under new and adverse conditions build up thier country and give it a place as the best section of this Great Country. How well they have done the work let the Forty five years since Appomatox; and present conditions speak; and tell of thier achivements in peace; as in War.

Notes

1. The title is from William McComb to R.T. Mockbee, February 16, 1911, Eleanor S. Brockenbrough Library, The Museum of the Confederacy.

2. Capt. June Kimble, "Tennesseeans At Gettysburg—The Retreat," *Confederate Veteran*, vol. 18 (October 1910), p. 463.

3. This was the claim of W.F. Fulton, "Archer's Brigade at Cold Harbor," *Confederate Veteran*, vol. 31 (August 1923), p. 300.

4. While in camp near Orange Court House, Virginia, on March 31, 1864, Col. William McComb wrote a skeletal history of the regiment. It is reprinted on pages 203-205 of *Tennesseans In The Civil War* (Nashville: Civil War Centennial Commission, 1964).

5. C. Wallace Cross, Jr., *Ordeal By Fire: A History of the Fourteenth Tennessee Volunteer Infantry Regiment, C.S.A.* (Clarksville, TN, 1990). The book covers the history of the regiment through the battle of Falling Waters (July 14, 1863) and includes a roster of the regiment. While the book is based almost exclusively on primary sources, including Robert Mockbee's historical sketch, it is marred by substantive errors in transcription and citation.

6. Biographies of McComb in Ezra J. Warner, *Generals in Gray* (Baton Rouge, 1964), pp. 198-199; William C. Davis, ed. *The Confederate General* (Harrisburg, 1991), vol. 4, pp. 112-113.

7. William McComb, "Tennesseeans in the Mountain Campaign, 1861," *Confederate Veteran*, vol. 22 (May 1914), p. 212.

8. Gustavus W. Dyer and John Trotwood Moore, compilers, *The Tennessee Civil War Veterans Questionnaires*, volume 4 (Easley, S.C., 1985), pp. 1554-1557. Compiled Service Record of R.T. Mockbee in Compiled Service Records of Confederate Soldiers. . .from Tennessee, National Archives microfilm series M-268, roll 176.

9. Cross, *Ordeal*, p. 12, says June 12; McComb, in Tennesseans, p.203, wrote that the regiment was organized in Clarksville on June 6th, then ordered to Nashville.

10. McComb in "Tennesseeans in the Mountain Campaign," , p. 210, and R. E. McCulloch, "Fourteenth Tennessee Infantry" (typescript of undated manuscript, Eleanor S. Brockenbrough Library, The Museum of the

Confederacy), p. 1, specified that those days were spent in Hainesville.

11. This is the first of several sub-section headings in Mockbee's manuscript. Mockbee centered only one of them, but the editors have, for reasons of clarity, chosen to center all of them.

12. Samuel R. Anderson had been lieutenant colonel of the 1st Tennessee Volunteers in Mexico. Gov. Isham Harris appointed him major general of Tennessee Volunteers, and he entered Confederate service as brigadier general. Warner, *Generals,* pp. 10-11; Davis, ed., *Confederate General,* vol. I, pp. 34-35. The Brigade was assigned to Gen Wm Loring's Division.

13. The campaign turned out to be a "complete failure," McComb *(Confederate Veteran,* p. 210) later remembered, thought it had begun as "a complete success." McComb deemed the plan of attack "admirable," and blamed its failure on the inexplicable failure of the forces on the eastern side of the mountain to attack.

14. In describing the Cheat Mountain campaign, McCulloch (pp. 1-2) wrote that "no tongue or pen has yet, or even can, set forth in their true colorings the privations, hardships, and sufferings endured by the troops on this memorable march over the trackless mountains."

15. Cross, *Ordeal,* pp. 17-18, citing letter of Lt. I.W. Howard, Co. G, lists clothing and other items received in camp.

16. McComb, *Confederate Veteran,* p. 211, remembered that Jackson had at first suggested that the men ford the river that night. Instead, over the next two days, the men labored in the cold by shifts building a log bridge across the Potomac.

17. Roster in Cross, *Ordeal,* confirmed that William H. Frazier of Richmond, Virginia, was discharged for wounds received at Hancock, Maryland. The roster cites also a letter dated March 25, 1863 explaining that Frazier was detailed to escorting Federal deserters from Liberty, Tennessee, to McMinnville, Tennessee; it was apparently then that he got into the trouble Mockbee described.

18. Lt. Col. Gholson had resigned his commission during the winter.

19. Col. Peter Turney's 1st Tennessee Infantry was technically the 1st Confederate Infantry Regiment or the 1st Tennessee Volunteer Infantry. After the transfer of Col. George Maney's 1st Tennessee Infantry (along with two other Tennessee regiments) to the west in January, Turney's regiment became known as the 1st Tennessee Infantry. *Tennesseans in the War,* pp. 170-173.

20. The 58-year-old Anderson resigned after the battle, but he was not under a cloud when he did so. In his report of the battle of West Point (Eltham's Landing), Gen. William Whiting (*Official Records,* series I, vol. XI, part 1, pp. 629-30) credited Anderson with arriving on the field "at a critical moment to the support of General Hood," putting two of his regiments into action and graciously waiving command on the field to Hood.

21. H.T. Childs, "The Battle of Seven Pines," *Confederate Veteran,* 24

(January 1917), p. 19, quotes Hatton's speech to troops before battle: "We are the only representatives of the gallant little commonwealth of Tennessee upon the soil of Virginia. I appeal to you as Tennesseeans. Show yourselves worthy sons of a noble ancestry."

22. Regimental casualty figures for the Seven Days, published in the July 22, 1862 Clarksville Chronicle, were reprinted in Confederate Veteran ("Fourteenth Tennessee Regiment," vol. 4, August 1896, p. 263) and in Cross, *Ordeal,* pp. 64-65.

23. An account of the 14th Tennessee at Second Manassas (Theo. Hartman, "With Jackson at Second Manassas") appeared in *Confederate Veteran,* 24 (December 1916), p. 557.

24. In his only published article on the war, Mockbee ("Why Sharpsburg Was a Drawn Battle," *Confederate Veteran,* 16[April 1908], p. 160) elaborated on his belief that Hill and his division had not received sufficient credit for its role at Sharpsburg.

25. Mockbee failed to mention that he was the man detailed from Company B. He was absent from the regiment on detached service between January 29 and May 7, 1863. Mockbee's account of the battle of Chancellorsville was not, therefore, written with the benefit of personal experience. R.T. Mockbee, Compiled Service Record.

26. For another account of the Tennesseans at Chancellorsville, see John Hurst, "Archer's Brigade at Chancellorsville," *Confederate Veteran* 7 (1899), p. 261.

27. There is no corroboration for this claim. In his report of the battle (*Official Records,* series I, vol. 25, part 1, p. 886), Hill credited Archer's brigade with capturing four guns, but singled out Brig. Gen. Stephen Ramseur's brigade for special commendation.

28. Sgt. Thomas C. Davidson of Clarksville, had been captured at Fredericksburg and released. He was captured again at Gettysburg. Secretary of War James Seddon promoted Davidson to Ensign on April 20, 1864 for gallantry at Chancellorsville and Gettysburg. Roster in Cross, Ordeal indicates that Davidson was taken prisoner on July 1st.

29. Sgt. Columbus J. Horn of Clarksville enlisted in Company G in May 1861 at the age of 26. He received a gunshot wound to the face at Gettysburg. He was promoted to 4th Sgt. on September 1, 1864. Roster in Cross, *Ordeal.* Casualty list in McCulloch indicates that Horn was killed at Petersburg in 1865.

30. Capt. June Kimble wrote in *Confederate Veteran* (p. 461) that the men of Archer's Brigade held the line for five to ten minutes and the prayed for support. When the support did not come many of the men surrendered rather than retreat across the field and "run the gauntlet of the enemy's fire." Upon returning to the Confederate lines many of the men were placed on picket duty in case the enemy attacked. Kimble estimated that about 100 of the 14th Tennessee's 350 men survived the assault. Robert K. Krick, in *The Gettysburg Death Roster* (Dayton, 1981), p. 14, estimated the

regiment's casualties for the entire battle at 127.

31. Kimble learned later that only 3 of the 86 troopers (a contingent from the 4th Michigan Cavalry) returned to Federal lines.

32. In his account of the regiment's activities in 1864-1865, McComb recalled skirmishing with enemy cavalry near Mount Crawford and occasional jousting as the Federal cavalry probed toward Staunton.

33. McComb was wounded at Chancellorsville.

34. Published as "The South Before and At The Battle of the Wilderness" (Richmond, 1878).

35. R.E. McCulloch (p. 6) wrote in similarly boastful terms: "Here [at the Wilderness] this gallant band stood in line of battle, without rest, for eighteen hours, beating back the forces of the enemy hurled against it."

36. In his account of the battle ("Recollections" of 1864-1865, Eleanor S. Brockenbrough Library, The Museum of the Confederacy, pp. 3-5. Hereinafter cited as "Recollections."), William McComb expressed pride in the regiment's execution of an order ("to change front to rear on left company and deploy to two paces front") on the afternoon of May 5th when it was discovered that the Federal line flanked the Confederate line. McComb also wrote that Gen. A.P. Hill told him that Lee assured him that "Longstreet would take his place on the front line before day" and that McComb, therefore, should "let the boys lie down and rest." Vaguely critical of Longstreet, McComb also admitted frankly that the men of the Tennessee brigade fell back in disorder when the Federal attack penetrated their line. McComb concluded that Longstreet's counterattack was more effective as a result of the Federals' initial success and concluded sarcastically: "So this was one time it was fortunate Longstreet was a little late coming into the fight."

37. McComb, "Recollections," pp. 5-7, wrote a detailed account of the regiment's roles in the battles of May 12 and May 19 at Spotsylvania.

38. The regiment received the order to drive Federal cavalry back across the North Anna near Howlett's Station as they were bathing and cooking a few miles away. "The Boys were not in a very good humer. You might Say they were fighting mad," wrote William McComb, "Recollections," p.7.

39. McComb, "Recollections," wrote a detailed account of the regiment's participation at Cold Harbor, dwelling especially on the dislodging of enemy sharpshooters from an "old house" in its front before the Federal attack.

40. McComb, "Recollections," p. 11, described the winter as "farely quiet" and noted that soldiers on both sides seemed less likely to shoot at a foe than they had been during the first year of the war.

41. Mockbee suffered his own personal "trials" during that winter. He was admitted to Chimborazo Hospital #4 with chronic diarrhea on October 1, 1864, remained in the hospital for three weeks and received a 30-day furlough on October 20th. He returned to the unit and was present for the January-February 1865 muster. Mockbee Service Record.

42. McComb, "Recollections," pp. 12-13, described the confusion of the night of April 1-2 as the Confederate line collapsed. The Tennessee brigade blunted the enemy advance and even launched a counter charge. "We had more prisoners than we had men in our command," McComb wrote.

"What I know I know, and I dare express it":

Major Raleigh S. Camp's History of the 40th Georgia Infantry in the Vicksburg Campaign

"It is not my object to write a History of the War. I leave that task to more skilled and abler pens," insisted Maj. Raleigh Spinks Camp when he began a memoir sometime in 1863. "My purpose is to place upon Record the journeyings and incidents connected with the 40th Ga. Regiment." He titled his record "The first campaign of the 40th Georgia, By an Officer of the Regiment. With an Appendix containing an account of the Seige [sic.] and Surrender of the Garrison at Vicksburg in a Series of letters." He planned to include in his record complete lists of the men of the regiment, casualties and changes and "A chapter on Anecdotes and Incidents that cannot fail to amuse those who once enjoyed them." While he did not apparently write a chapter of amusing incidents and anecdotes, Camp compiled a list of the regiment's members with notations of changes and casualties incurred between March 1862 and March 1863. He transcribed the list from the company rolls on April 1, 1863, about the time that he wrote a history (61 double-spaced pages transcribed) of the 40th Georgia's first campaign.

At some time after July 1863, Camp wrote the "appendix" of letters detailing the regiment's experiences in the Vicksburg campaign and siege. These are not actually letters written from the field. They may be transcriptions of letters sent to an unspecified correspondent, after-the-fact recollections written as letters or letters reconstructed from diary notes. The letters and the memoir of the 40th Georgia's first campaign were, however, essentially wartime documents, since Raleigh Spinks Camp died in November 1867 before he had an opportunity to finish writing and arranging his carefully prepared record.

Camp's papers represent the most complete known memoir of the 40th Georgia.[1] The only other eyewitness account was written in 1911 by Pvt. Joseph Bogle, a source which its modern editors admitted was "sketchy" and limited.[2] Bogle offered little detail on the regiment's first campaign, was recuperating from a wound for the latter half of 1863 and spent the last ten months of the war in a Federal prison camp. Aside from a few recollections about the 1864 Atlanta Campaign, Bogle's *Recollections* is essentially the chapter of anecdotes and incidents which Raleigh Camp never wrote.

Camp, in contrast, wrote nothing about the regiment's experience after its surrender at Vicksburg in July 1863, but in great detail about the regiment's first year of the war and its experiences at Vicksburg. The regiment was formed in March 1862 from companies raised in five northwest Georgia counties. It was one of six Georgia regiments organized and sent almost immediately to Maj. Gen. Edmund Kirby Smith's Army of East Tennessee. Though initially scattered among several brigades, five of the new Georgia regiments, including the 40th, were in December 1862 formed into a brigade commanded by a Virginia-born West Point graduate, Brig. Gen. Seth Barton, and assigned to the division of Maj. Gen. Carter L. Stevenson. Those five regiments remained brigaded together for the remainder of the war, first under Barton, then, after Vicksburg, under command of Brig. Gen. Marcellus Stovall in Maj. Gen. Henry D. Clayton's division, Lieut. Gen. Alexander P. Stewart's corps, Army of Tennessee.

In "The first campaign," Camp detailed the regiment's movements in defense of Cumberland Gap, its first action at Tazewell, Tennessee (August 6, 1862), its participation in the October 1862 invasion of Kentucky and its transferral to Vicksburg in time to participate in the battle of Chickasaw Bluffs in late December 1862. In addition to narrating events, great and small, Camp recorded his own colorful opinions about political conditions, most notably the unionist sentiment in East Tennessee, the inauguration of Richard Hawes as the pro-Confederate governor of Kentucky and the failure of Kentucky's citizens to support the invading Southern army. It was sickness and death from disease (primarily measles) which preoccupied Camp the most in his account

Maj. Raleigh Camp
The Museum of the Confederacy

of the 40th Georgia's first year. Of the 183 men who died, Camp reckoned that 177 had died from disease, four were killed in action and two had died from accidents. The loss represented 16 1/4 per cent of the regiment's original strength.

When, at the end of that first campaign, Raleigh Camp determined to chronicle the services of the 40th Georgia, he was well placed and qualified for the task.[3] Born in Waltonville, Georgia, in 1829, Camp came to the regiment with significant education and military experience. He graduated from the Georgia Military Institute in Marietta, then returned to the school as a professor of mathematics. In 1859, he married Laura Clifford Jones, by whom Camp had a son and a daughter. On the eve of the war Camp moved to Texas to begin a law practice. There he became captain of Company B of the 7th Texas Infantry. He served with that unit in Kentucky and Tennessee and was absent sick when the regiment was surrendered at Fort Donelson in February 1862. An officer without a regiment, Camp returned to Georgia and was promptly commissioned major of the newly-formed 40th Georgia.

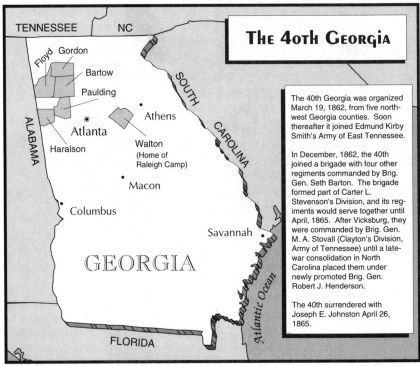

THE 40TH GEORGIA

The 40th Georgia was organized March 19, 1862, from five northwest Georgia counties. Soon thereafter it joined Edmund Kirby Smith's Army of East Tennessee.

In December, 1862, the 40th joined a brigade with four other regiments commanded by Brig. Gen. Seth Barton. The brigade formed part of Carter L. Stevenson's Division, and its regiments would serve together until April, 1865. After Vicksburg, they were commanded by Brig. Gen. M. A. Stovall (Clayton's Division, Army of Tennessee) until a late-war consolidation in North Carolina placed them under newly promoted Brig. Gen. Robert J. Henderson.

The 40th surrendered with Joseph E. Johnston April 26, 1865.

Mark A. Moore

With his background, Camp found himself detailed to a succession of administrative posts: brigade provost marshall (May-July 1862), provost marshall and commander of the post of Tazewell (August-September 1862), and brigade inspector general (appointed January 12, 1863). Camp held the post which his men dubbed "Fault finding General" throughout the Vicksburg campaign. For part of the campaign, Camp also commanded the regiment, as Col. Abda Johnson commanded the brigade in Seth Barton's absence.

Following the Vicksburg campaign and the parole and exchange of the regiment's members, the 40th Georgia and Raleigh Camp joined Maj. Gen. Braxton Bragg's Army of Tennessee. It participated in the Chattanooga campaign in the fall of 1863, fought in nearly action of the 1864 Atlanta campaign.[4] and was with the army to its surrender on April 26, 1865.

While he was still in the service, Raleigh Camp was not with the 40th Georgia during its final year of campaigning. Camp was wounded at the battle of Marietta, Georgia, on May 23, 1864, and had his wounded left arm amputated. Confined to a hospital with a 45-day furlough, Camp returned to the army and was in command of the regiment at least in August and September 1864.[5] The final month of the war found him acting as engineering officer for the Department of North Georgia. He was paroled in Kingston, Georgia, in May 1865. Camp attempted to resume his life in Texas, not as a lawyer, but as agent for the Knickerbocker Life Insurance Company. He died of "congestion of the brain" (meningitis) in November 1867. He was buried in Atlanta, but his remains were moved in 1900 to Oak Hill Cemetery, Birmingham, Alabama, where his wife subsequently settled.

Published here without abridgement are Camp's Vicksburg "letters" and those portions of "The first campaign" pertaining to the regiment's activities at Vicksburg. Camp was well educated, and wrote with extraordinarily colorful language (some would say verbosity). Consistent with James McPherson's assertion that Civil War soldiers were deeply ideological,[6] Camp was a fervent believer in the Confederate cause and interjected many observations on the cause into his letters. This transcription retains original spelling and punctuation, errors and all (most notably the consistent misspellings of their as "thier" artillery with one "l" and omitting the "e" in verbs ending in "ed"). Annotations are minimal, so as to allow publication of his entire account of the 40th Georgia at Vicksburg.

≈ ≈ ≈

On Saturday the 27th Dec 1862 at 11 oc. A.M. The Regiment reached the Depot at Vicksburg having been pent up on the cars a week. the men were necessarily much fatigued and jaded. But there was no time now for rest as the Enemy had on this day engaged Genl [Stephen Dill] Lee on Chickasaw Bayou about four miles above the city on the Valley Road. The Enemy had gone up the Yazoo and landed below Snyders Bluff and intended to go into Vicksburg at the Back door, or in other words to force thier way and get in possession of the line of our Breastworks and fortifications. At 1 oc. P.M. our Regt. was ordered to march to Mint Spring about 1 1/2 or 3 miles North of the City. The Regt. reached this place late in the evening and lay down to rest as best they in the cold without tents. They were not permitted to enjoy thier repose long for about 12 oc at night. They got orders to march out on the Valley Road which they did and stopped in the Road on the left of Gen Lee's Brigade. All was now quiet along the lines and the Men were lying about in the Road and in the fence corners and some of them to make themselves more comfortable made up small fires to keep themselves warm. At about 4 oc. in the morning the silence was disturbed by the salute of the Artilery of the Enemy and the deadly missile scattered the fuel at one of the fires where a crowd was seated. The fires were extinguised without orders. The men prefering darkness to light on this occasion at least; and not feeling the better for being aroused by this novel and unusual style of Revielle. The Enemy had taken his position on the west bank of the Bayou, about 700 yards in our front; and from this point they kept up a heavy fire from thier Batteries. About sunrise the Enemy having crossed the Bayou, attacked Gen Lee's Brigade and the fight with them continued the whole day, Gen Lee holding his position against thier charges.

The 40th was kept as a reserve to Support the 31st La Regt (Col Morrison) which was in the trenches in front of the Indian Mound Who was also attacked at Sunrise by the Enemy; About 2 oc. P.M. Col. Morrison sent to Col. Johnson[8] for help to hold his position. Col. Johnson first sent him Co. A. (Lieut [Franklin A.M.]Boyd) Co B (Lieut [Edward or Edmond] Fort[d]) Co. C (Lieut [A.M.] Carter) Co. D (Capt [Francis H.] Hall) & Co. E. (Capt [J.F.] Groover). About 3 oc. P.M. Col Johnson sent Co's G & F also. The three remaining companies remained in the Road. The enemy fought at this point until 8 or 9 oc. when finding that he could not drive our men from thier position, ceased his fire and all was quiet. Thus ended the first day of the Chickasaw fight and nothing was decided except the very important fact that the Enemy had found the side down to the Hill City a little more closely watched than he had supposed, and that to enable him to enter he must tread the threshold with a stronger force. The loss in our Regt. today was small. [A.A.] Gray of Co. D[9] and [Pvt. J. D.] Kikes of Co. F. were killed early in the day. And Col Johnson was slightly wounded in the shoulder by a cannon shot.

— 29th Dec 1862

~ All was quiet during the night. But at day light the Enemy opened the fight with renewed vigor and a determination to dislodge us or die. Consequently the yell was raised and the charge ordered. They are mowed down and deranged. They form and come on again. They are met by Lee's Brigade (the 42d Ga. Regt. Within) The Enemy halt and about 500 of them Surrender and are led off Prisoners. They make a desperate charge upon the 31st Ga. and 40th Ga. but are repulsed with heavy loss. Thus passed off the Second and last day of the fight. The Enemy had brought all his forces and they [illegible] to do this days work and had been driven back. Thier Officers had ranted and raved, persuaded and threatened, but all in vain, and to no purpose. They found that the "In to Vicksburg" was a hard road to travel. and that they could not make the trip, and that they must give it up as a bad job, thus delaying thier visit until a more convenient Season.

Hence at night the Enemy withdrew his forces and fell back to thier boats on the Yazoo leaving his dead and wounded upon the Battle field. Today [Pvt. W.G.] Gann of Co A.[10] and [Pvt. James A.] Roach of Co C. were killed and some others Slightly wounded. The loss on our side was small as compared with that of the Enemy as our men were generally in the trenches. The casualties on either side I have not yet seen.[11]

— 30th Dec 1863

~ To day the Enemy sent over a flag of Truce and got permission to burry thier dead and attend to thier wounded, which duty they discharged in front of our fortications and under our bayonets.

The Regt continued in the trenches exposed to rain and cold for several days until it was certain that the Enemy would not renew the attack again. They then went in camp at Mint Spring and continued there until about the last of January.

Thus has the Regt passed through the second fight with but little suffering. All behaved like men and like soldiers; and if they did not suffer more, or do more, it was no fault of thiers. The Yankees being foiled in thier attempt to take the city, fell back on the west bank of the Mississippi River, made thier encampment near the Head of thier bayous Canal, and with thier dredge Boats began to work upon thier ditch again. I believe that it is generally given up that if Barton's Brigade had not arrived at the time it did that the Enemy would have dislodged Gen. Lee. and thus have taken the Stronghold Vicksburg. This fact is believed by all in the Brigade. And though the Genl Commanding has never said, officially as much, yet it is believed and any thing me may do or omit will not change the mind or remove the impression. It is fixed - tis founded on truth.

The 40th has never fought for Glory, nor has She been trumpeted in the papers for any of her acts. They are content to do thier duty as soldiers and as men When they are conscious that they have "acted well thier part." They know "where the honor lies." And General Orders, to inscribe Vicksburg or anything else upon thier Banner cannot add to or detract from the merit that belongs to her. The following Order No. 72 was published. It only pays Col. [Robert J.] Henderson and his noble Regt. a fit compliment.[12] They deserve it. And there is not a man in the Brigade but who is glad to see that at least one Ga. Regt. was known by the Lieut. Genl. to be in the Battle that saved Vicksburg. But why the 40th, 43d & 52d Ga. Regts. which were in the fight are not noticed is not for me to say.[13] The actions of some men are not easily explained.

≈ ≈ ≈

Headquarter Department Mississippi and East Louisiana,
VICKSBURG, MISS., May 13th 1863
GENERAL ORDERS, NO. 72

In honor to the troops engaged in the fight near Vicksburg, on the 29th day of December, 1862, and in commemoration of thier gallant and meritorious conduct on that occasion, the following commands will inscribe upon thier standards "VICKSBURG" - viz:

17th Regt. La. Vols.;
26th " " "
28th " " "
3d Reg't Tenn. Vols.;
30th " " "
80th " " "
Co. "A", 1st Reg't Miss. Light Artillery;
Co. "D", " " " "
    42nd Reg't Ga. Vols.
    By order of
    Lieut.-Gen. PEMBERTON
    R.W. Memminger
    A.A.G.[14]

— Jan. 1863

~ The time was spent at the Camp near Chickasaw Bayou in drawing Rations and getting wood, and keeping good fires as the weather was cold.

About the 28th our wagons and horses arrived having been on the road Six weeks. We were glad to see them as our transportation had been very limited The men were compelled to carry Meal & Beef three miles on thier shoulders, or as the Texans would call it "Rack".

On the 29th we got orders to move 1 1/2 miles below Vicksburg on the Warrenton Road, at Camp Reeve which has been our base of operations ever since. It is a very good Camp having all the conveniences that can be expected at the time to wit: wood water &c. It was about the 28th that Col. Johnson was put in command of the Brigade, Gen Barton having Command at Warrenton. The Col. continued in Comd of the Brigade until about the 10th of May giving satisfaction to all parties either above or below him. The men were now engaged in drilling and perfecting themselves in other duties that they had never had an opportunity to learn, And every 5th day they went to Warrenton on Picket duty to watch the Yankees as it was supposed they would attempt to land in force at that point. We saw several exciting scenes, as we were near the River. When the Gun Boats ran the gauntlet under the fire of our

Batteries [April 16, 1863] we were marched to the trenches with the first gun fired and witnessed the cannonading which was at night. It was truly grand and Terrific. We will never forget those sights.

On the 12th Major Camp was appointed Inspector General of the Brigade or as the Boys call him the Fault finding General. His success at improving the Military and police discipline is well known to all. And the First Sgts. particularly, As they had good reason to believe that he was strict to the letter and "Riggid to the Law".

The Regiment was never as strong and efficient as at this time. the Ranks were generally full, the men in splendid health and fine spirits And generally enjoyed themselves as well as soldiers can.[15]

≈ ≈ ≈

An *Appendix* Containing an account
from the Battle near Port Gibson
to the Surrender of the Garrison at Vicksburg

In a Series of Letters
By R.S. Camp
Major 40th Georgia Infantry

No. 1
Near Warrenton, Miss.
5th May 1863

My Dear Sir-
You have doubtless heard, that after the Yankees were foiled in thier attempt to take Vicksburg by way of Yazoo Road and Sunflower, He then turned his attention to the South, or Port Gibson plan. And during the latter part of April it was known that the Enemy was landing his forces above Vicksburg and marching them down on the West side of the River near Port Gibson and there by means of Transports that run by our Batteries, a short time since, were crossed over on the Mississippi Side. Port Gibson is a small town about 35 miles below Vicksburg. About 10 miles

above Port Gibson is Grand Gulf at the Mouth of Big Black River. Our Batteries at this point, had up to this time protected, or kept the Enemy's Boats out of this River.

Gen. Pemberton knowing that the Enemy were thus getting a foot hold on this side of the River sent three Brigades, towit, Gen. Bowen's, Green's (known as the 1st and 2nd Missouri) and Gen. Tracy's (Ala) to dislodge the Enemy. On Friday the 1st of May our forces attacked the Enemy at Bayou Pierre, and after a long and bloody engagement our forces were overpowered and driven back with heavy loss. Our loss in killed wounded and prisoners amounting to about 2,000. Among the killed was Brigaders Gen. [Edward D.] Tracy, a noble and Gallent officer. Col [D.R.] Hundley of the 31st Ala. was wounded and fell into the hands of the Enemy. Andersons Battery which has been with our Regt so long was in the fight and Suffered very much. Four pieces of the six were captured by the Enemy. Lieuts [Philip] Peters & [William Price] Douth[a]t, were both killed by one shot, and Lieut [William H.] Norgr[a]ve is supposed to be killed. This is sad, as it is the first battle this splendid Battery has been engaged in, And the death of these three heroic officers pains all who were acquainted with them, and especially those of us who had been associated with them for the last year. And knew thier noble and gentlemanly qualities so well. Truly none more have ere Mand a Gun.[16] The grand mistake of sending a mere handful of men to meet an army- a Mole hill against a Mountain- was, now, when too late, discovered. Hence on Friday evening reinforcements and among them the 40th Ga were ordered to march. Our brigade went down to Warrenton Friday Night. On Saturday evening we left Warrenton and marched nearly all night crossing Big Black just before day at Hankersons's Ferry, which is about 14 miles from Warrenton. before day our forces had crossed the River and marched some five or six miles, and formed in line of Battle, expecting to be attacked by the Enemy. But we did not remain here long before order were received to fall back across the River, which was done, and at night we campd about three miles this side of the Ferry. It was evident now that the Enemy had made, and would hold his point. Early this morning the Guns were spiked, the Magazine blown up, and our position at Grand Gulf evacuated. thus giving the Enemy Big Black. The fact now that

Gen. Grant had out generaled our Gen. was too evident. And both officers and men showed in thier countenances that Matters were not being managed to our advantage. All saw that the Anaconda was getting his deadly grasp upon us and that ere long, unless something is done, he will encircle Vicksburg within his iron folds. To break which will require mighty strokes.

On Monday we fell back to Warrenton. Our line extending from Warrenton to Bovina on the Southern Rail Road. The 40th was stationed and is now stationed at Glass'line about 3 miles below Warrenton on the River, as a picket to watch the movements of the Enemy in case he attempts a landing. One of thier Gun boats is in the River just below us. I presume that is it for a watch and a signal. As I have no idea that the Enemy will try to land at this point. I think it probable that he will move up the Big Black towards Jackson, take possession the Rail Road, and thus cut off our communication and supplies, and then cross the river and either give us battle or circumvoltate us within the narrow confines of our trenches. The time passes on, and no Enemy approaches, except the Gun Boat came up the Batteries at Warrenton this morning, and belched forth her deadly missiles, and then moved off with as much impudence as a Yankee indeed. Rumors are afloat that the enemy are advancing towards the Rail Road. All are now daily in expectation of Stirring times, And you need not be surprised any day to hear of a battle. The Military Weathercock plainly points to such a thing. For the present I will close with the promise that I will keep you posted as to passing events in this vicinity. I am yours truly

R. S. Camp

No. 2
Near Edward's Depot
Friday 15th May 1863

My Dear Sir-

When I wrote you ten days ago I was at Warrenton, We remained there until last Tuesday evening when we received orders to march immediately - We left Glass'line about 4 oc P.M. and started in the direction of Rail Road Bridge on the Big Black River. We marched all night and just a day halted near Mount

Abion Church and lay on the Road side and slept. the best we could do for about two hours; Then under a hot and burning sun we started and about 10 oc. we reached Bovina Station on the Rail Road. About 1 oc. P.M. we reached the River. The men fatigued and broken down.

Here we learned that all the forces had crossed the River and that our Brigade Barton's was in the rear. We remained on the bank of the River until nearly night, and leaving parties to cook, we crossed the River and marched on in the direction of the Depot. Edwards Depot is six miles from the River. we reached the depot about 10 oc. P.M. and going on about one Mile East of the Depot we were put in line of Battle, and here we campd, This morning (Thursday) it is raining and all is at a stand still. The Genls of our Army are convened today I presume for the purpose of Providing the best ways and and means to meet the Enemy who is now in a short distance and reported 60,000 Strong. On Friday morning all is quiet- at the time I write- Everything now indicates that there is work ahead. The Enemy has advanced his forces to the Rail Road. He has taken Clinton and Jackson, and is now threatening to move his main body in the direction of Vicksburg. It is very certain that he cares nothing for Jackson or any other point in this section, only when the reduction of such points will strengthen his efforts to take the Hill City. Word is brought in that the Enemy is between this and Raymond, and Rumor is that Gen. Johnston is advancing to meet us and that we will join him before the fight comes on. About 10 oc. M. we have orders to march, and the army is put in motion in the direction of the Enemy in the following order 1st Loring's Division, 2d Bowes's and 3d Stevenson's. As it will be nearly night before our Regiment starts, I will have ample time to finish my letter. It is now clear that an engagement is inevetable, and the question arises are we prepared for it. The Enemy is said to be much stronger than we are. The bravery of the Western Army has never been questioned. The have shown themselves to be good fighters. I would like to feel cheerful and hopeful, but I cannot. I feel the burthen of heavy gloom resting upon me. I see dispair depicted upon the faces of our soldiers, which I construe as an ill omen. The 40th is now on the march. I will write you again soon. Yours Truly.

R.S. Camp

No. 3
11/2 Miles West of Big Black
Sunday morning 17th May 1863

My Dear Sir-

When I closed my last the army was in motion on the Raymond Road. They marched on about 5 or 6 miles, crossed Baker's Creek and stoped about midnight about 2 miles East of said creek, and formed in line of Battle. Early on Saturday (16th) The skirmishers began to give signals that the two armies were near each other. After crossing the creek and going about 2 miles our army had taken a Right hand, or road running due South. Our left resting at the junction of the two Roads, which is about 3 miles from Bolton's Station, and near the Residence of Mr. Champion.[17] As the morning grew up the Pickets became more and more engaged. The Wagons which had been carried to this place were now ordered to fall back and another such a Hustle and Bustle as you never saw. Quarter Masters directing and drivers cussing and whipping thier teams made a sight and confusion that is not very pleasant to witness at any time.

About ten oclock the Enemy's signal fire on our left threw its column of smoke high among the hills. Soon after one on our right also loomed up in the distance. The sharpshooters now became generally engaged on the left or near the forks of the Road. At about 11 oc. Lees Brigade which had been ordered back to the Raymond Road, or the Junction, became closely engaged. The fight was now raging with fury on this Brigade, on our extreme left, And still the Gen. commanding was slow to send reinforcements. But about 12 M. when Lees Brigade had begun to give way owing to the large force brought against it, Cummings Brigade was ordered to its left, instead to its support. It was not long before Lee was crushed and his Brigade forced to fall back in disorder. The Enemy then came down on Cumming.

At this time Barton's, or our Brigade, was ordered to the left of Cumming. We were formed in line of battle on his left about 12 1/2 M. But we had hardly formed before Cumming was overpowered, and his Brigade routed and they were falling back in confusion. About 1 oc. P.M. Gen. Barton and his Staff gave the order to charge the Enemy - and mark you, the Enemy could not be seen

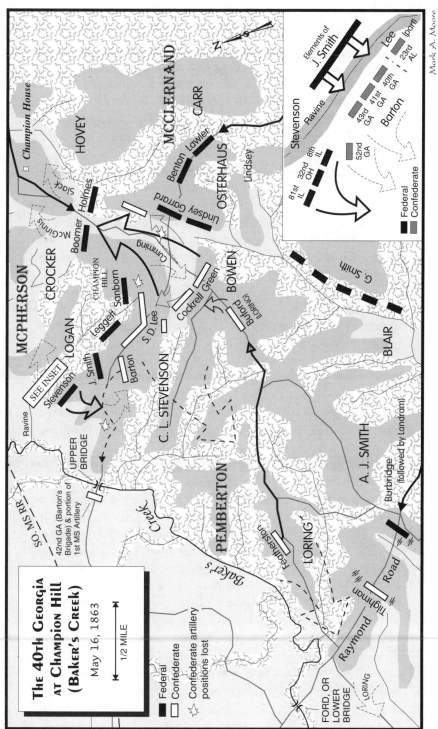

The 40th Georgia
at Champion Hill
(Baker's Creek)

May 16, 1863

1/2 MILE

Federal
Confederate
Confederate artillery
positions lost

Mark A. Moore

in our front, even our skirmishers had not fired upon the Enemy.

We advanced in as good order as the roughness of the ground would permit, and at the distance of about 200 yards. The 40th formed and stopped in a Ravine, and here did her fighting. I was on Gen. Barton's staff, but he ordered me to go to the right of my Regiment and hold the point at all hazards. Col. Johnson was very sick and had been down for some days.[18] And just as the charge was ordered he rode down the road where the left of our Brigade rested and when the fight opened he made his way out under a most deadly fire. On our Right in the Ravine, was a part of the 23d Ala. which had been rallied and on our left the 41st Ga. Regt. The enemy was now but a short distance from us and the fight opened hot and heavy. I rode down to the right of the Regiment and gave all the directions necessary. after while Capt Foster reported that the ammunition was being exhausted. I then ordered a detail to be sent for some. During all this time, not a word could I hear from the Gen. I saw that the force upon our Right had fallen back. I had my horse at this time shot thro. the neck. I mounted and rode as near the left as I could get; but could see nothing of Lt. Col. Young. I now saw that the 41st had given way and were falling back. I then rode up to the Road where Col. Eustis was trying to Rally his Regt. and told him to caution his men to be particular as the 40th was still over the Hill. The Col. said he knew that, and that we had best fall back, as the Enemy were flanking us. I then went down to the Regt. again, and found that many of the men were out of ammunition and the Enemy pouring deadly fire upon them. I sent word to Adjt. Warnick, who was at the Center of the Regt. fighting with a musket (I could still see nothing of Col. Young, tho I could not see the left) that I took the responsibility to order the Regt. to fall back. I then went to the right and told Capts Foster & Neal the same. As the Regt. fell back from the Ravine, we suffered the most as we were exposed to the fire of the Enemy. I rode on ahead of the Regt. to see where they should go just before I got to the Road I heard a voice. "Halt you d—d Rebel". I looked down and on the ground where we had formed, before the charge, I saw the Yankees not exceeding 40 yards from me. Instead of halting I turned to the Regt and motioned them to turn up the hill. And then put spurs to my horse. The Yankees seeing that I did not obey them Fired a volly of Balls upon me - as thick as hail stones. I then thought that we might run into the Enemy on top of the hill, a distance of 150, so I made for that point, and when I got there I saw the way open for us to get into the field. You have no idea how much relieved I felt and I shouted to the Regt on the way was open. We then passed thro the field, crossed a Ravine and soon were mingling with the scattering fragments olf the other Regts. and other Brigades. The Yankees were pouring a deadly fire upon us all the time. At this time the Missouri Brigade had engaged the Enemy near the forks of the Road and drove him back; but the Enemy had gained his point. He had cut us off from the Road we came, and, if he had pushed up his victory would have cut off our retreat effectually. The 43d and 52d Ga Regts had been driven back in disorder before the 40th gave up her position. Col. [Alpheus Skidmore] Harris of the 43d was badly wounded and left on the field.[19] Col. [Charles D.] Phillips of the 52d was, it's said, mortally wounded, and left to the mercy of the foe.[20] The 42d Ga. before the fight began, was ordered to the bridge at Bakers Creek and doubtless the stand they made there held the Enemy in check until we made safe our retreat.

The demoralized Right now made thro the plantations and crossing Bakers Creek below got the Rail Road at Edward's Depot before the Enemy, that is, the bulk of them. Many were doubtless captured who could have got out if they had tried. Gen [William W.] Loring was ordered to protect the rear and bring it up with his division (8000 strong), But either from necessity or choice he did not come up And I hear that he is down on the other side of Big Black.

The Stampede in the evening and all night surpasses description and even the imagination of one who never witnessed the route of a demoralised and disorganised army. They are worse than a flock of Sheep without a shepherd. We need not talk of the Yankees flight at Bull Run. None can surpass this. Our troops were crossing the River all night last night. This morning the Enemy had closed upon us. Two Brigades Gen Green's Missouri and Gen Vaughn's Tenn. were ordered to meet them at the fortifications at the Bridge, But they did not stand long before the Enemy charged and drove them from thier position and our men forced to swim the River for safety. Thus ends the fight at Bakers Creek, in which we were outnumbered and crushed. Three Brigades of Stevenson's Division done nearly all the fighting and suffered the most. These three Brigades were met by six Divisions of the Enemy and only one Brigade fought at the same time, for the first was whipped before the others entered the fight. It is plain that the Enemy massed his forces on his right to turn our left and thus out Generaled our Commanders.

The great wonder is that we were not all captured to say nothing of our wagons. Our losses I do not know. I learn that yesterday and this morning we have lost 60 pieces of Artilery.[21] It is a complete triumph to the Enemy. The Rail Road Bridge is now on fire, and our poor Army is en route for Vicksburg to make the last stand. I must close. I will write you again. Excuse this hastily written letter. Yours truly.

R.S. Camp

P.S. I hope you will not charge me with Egotism for using the I concerning the fight. I only did my duty. The men & officers all say that had it not been for me the Regt would have been captured in five minutes. Which is so.

No. 4

Near Vicksburg

Wednesday 20th May 1863

My Dear Sir:

The smoke of the battle at Baker's Creek having somewhat cleared off, And we can now see a part of the effects. I have concluded to write you again. I was forced to close my last rather abruptly and take up the line of march for Vicksburg and Safety. I can now give you some idea of our loss. The casualties of the 40th Ga stand about thus, 175 killed, wounded and missing. Not more than 12 or 15 are known to be killed, about 40 wounded, the most of them came off the field; hence you see that our greatest loss are in prisoners.

In our Brigade the total loss is about 900 and our whole loss is not far from 3000, which is heavy, but it could have been far worse. We have to lament the death of Brig Gen Tilghman who was killed late Saturday evening. He was a noble and Gallent officer. Also the loss of Majr [Joseph W.] Anderson Chief of Artilery

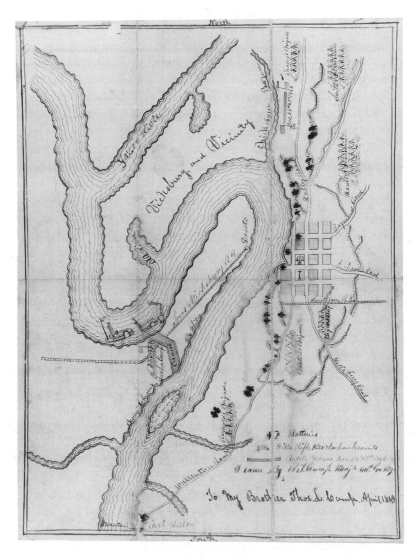

Hand-drawn map of Confederate lines at Vicksburg
The Museum of the Confederacy

in our Division. Than whom a braver and more true spirit never lived or died.

We have been charged by the Citizens and soldiers from other states, with cowardice. It has been frequently said, I hear, that the Georgians run. It is true they did run, but not till after they were forced. I can and will speak for the 40th Ga. She stood her ground until long after the line on her right and left was broken and had fallen back, And still she was loth to give up her position. And still she fell back in good order from the ground on which she fought. And still she is ready and willing to fight as long as any set of men. And still her officers and men behaved as becometh Georgians, and Patriots. And still we are called cowards. And <u>still</u>, I say, on the part of the Regt. that he who <u>says</u> that the 40th Ga. behaved in a manner unbecoming Soldiers and Gentlemen, on the 16th day of May 1863, at the battle of Baker's Creek, is a base and foul calumniater. Excuse me for using such language, but I must out with the truth. What I know I know, and I dare express it.[22]

I will now return to the condition and situation of our Army which on Sunday morning was making its way back to Vicksburg, and the Enemy at our heels. Everything now pointed to Vicksburg. Our crippled little Army looked to it as the only Haven of Safety now left them - The last place where they could hope to make a stand against a large and overwhelming army. flushed with victory and mad with the spirit of capture and conquest. The same relentless Foe who have been for 12 months Rolling Vicksburg under thier tongues as a sweet morsal, and have again and again tried to take the little city, and thus control the Great Mississippi, and crush the Rebelion, and have been as often met and repulsed by a handful of Rebels, are now on the heels of the Rebels and marching in at the Back door at double quick time, laying the flattering injunction to thier souls that they will make the <u>Trip</u> this time. In the evening our forces reached Vicksburg and were assigned thier places determined to hold them or die in the effort. The line of fortifications are on average about two miles from the City. The Right is down below the City on the Warrenton Road, Bartons Brigade has its position on the Right and the 40th Ga Regt is consequently on the right next to the River.

Early on Monday [May 18th] the Enemy made his appearance in front of our lines and began to fire upon us principly on the center, or near where the Jackson Road crosses the lines. They thought all they had to do was to raise the yell, and fire a few shots and our men would fly before or surrender, but in this they were mistaken for our men, in the trenches, bid defiance to them, hence they kept at a respectable distance during the day, keeping up a constant fire upon us. The Federal Army has closed around us and we are now beseiged. All communication with the outer world is now cut off. Every step is now taken to economise the Subsistince. And to this end our horses are not to have any more corn, and the daily Rations are reduced to one fourth. The calculations are made that we can live at this rate for 60 or 70 days. We hope to be able to hold the Enemy in check at our lines, And thus give our friends outside the time to relieve us. The Gun-Boats from below have moved up close by, and are in the ring to hold us fast. Above we see them also with many Transports. The Yankees have on the peninsula oposite the City a Battery of six heavy mortors from which they belch forth thier missiles. The weight of some of them is 200 lbs. With these they expect to finish the distinction of the City, Day and night this <u>Thunder</u> of Earth is roaming in its sad and "<u>Alaurem tones</u>."

To day (Wednesday) The Enemy finding that we were not to be frightened out of the trenches They concluded to come in by force, So They massed in front of Gen. Schaft's Brigade and made a charge upon the lines. Our men let them approach within close range and then let them have a volly which mowed them down. The Ranks were filled and on they came again, but with the same fate. They hesitate, fall back and give it up, leaving the ground covered with thier dead and wounded. They are now partially convinced, I presume, that the Rebels will give them some trouble yet before they get into the "Hill City". Our Soldiers are in fine spirits and are willing to forego any hardships to hold this place and still let the Rebel Flag float proudly over the "Battlements of the Brave". I will keep you posted on points here.

Your truly

R.S. Camp

P.S. In my last I mentioned that Gen Loring had not come up

with his Division. It was supposed that he would make his way
down to Hall's Ferry and there cross Big Black and join us at this
place. But he has not come and a Courior, just in, reports that he
made his way to Jackson and has joined Gen Joe Johnston. I omit-
ted also to state that our forces Evacuated Snyder's Bluff which is
twelve miles above this place on the Yazoo River. This will be of
great advantage to the Enemy as it will serve as his base of operations. They are now all around us and doubtless think that they
will get us everyone soon.

> No. 5   Bealeagured Camp
> Near Vicksburg Miss.
> Monday 25th May 1863

My Dear Sir:

On Wednesday last I closed my letter just on the eve of the
first charge, made by the Yankees on our lines. On Thursday they
were busily engaged arranging thier batteris on our front, in order to make one fell sweep - of noise - upon us. They kept up from
dawn till dark a continuous fire with thier artilery and sharp
shooter on our trenches. If a man looks over the parapets his
head is a target. The Yankees are also entrenching on our front.
Thier object is, I presume, to keep these filled with Sharp shooters
which will protect them, and they are at the same time can annoy
us very much. It may be thier intention to thus approach us by a
System of parrellels, I think they will find this a hard job.

On Friday the 22d They concluded that they must redeem
thier promise to "take Vicksburg" and be done with. The
Prisoners, captured, report that Grant had promised an honorable discharge and $200.00 Bounty to those who would charge
and break our lines. His infatuated hords could not stand this
temptation, and would not miss this chance to go home. Hence
on thier madness they began the bloody work. They massed and
made the onset upon Gen. Herbert's Brigade; as they came
yelling like so many "fiends from Hell", our men cool and deliber-
ate brought down each his man. They rally, and shouting D—d
the Rebels on they come, a blast from the Trenches, and thier
front is broken. But on they come. A smoke flashes over the
Embankment, and hundreds of the Blue coats bite the dust. Rage

now burns with fury. Not a voice is heard in our trenches, save a low but earnest voice, "Keep cool boys, wait for the word and shoot low. Out side, the grons of the dying, the shrieks of the wounded, and the <u>War Cry</u> of the Enemy, mingle in one discordant storm of death and destruction. Thier Ranks move up to our lines, like the surges of the Mighty Deep against the Rocky Beach. The word "<u>Fire</u>" reverberates along our lines, and many of the living ly down in the dust and welter in blood beside thier dying comrades. A few reach the Embankments. They shout! They Mout [?], and plant thier colers. But soon they fall to rise no more.

Thier Leaders, now in despair, with curses and threats order the <u>Onward</u> again. The men hesitate and cry out. Tis no Battle, but Slaughter and death. They move on again. Another Rebel Volley and the Yankees turn and fly in disorder. The living fall back in disgrace and dispair, leaving thier comrades discharged on the ground, and sent to a home (H-l) which doubtless they will find a few degrees <u>warmer</u> than Dixie.

I think they are now converted to our <u>Faith</u> which we proclaim daily on our lines and which is couched in the language of our old. "Stay thy proud waves, thus far, and no farther, shalt thou come". Tho they may be Infidels enough to try it again. I do not know thier losses have been in these attempts, to break our lines: but it certainly was heavy. Our loss was comparatively small.

A party of Yankees succeedd to get into a gully about 50 yards in front of Gen Lee's Brigade and both they and our men were afraid to raise thier heads to shoot or to advance upon each other. Nor could the Yankees get out without being exposed to a deadly fire. Gen Lee demanded a surrender. They refused and defied him. He then sent off and procured some shells which he charged and fired the fuse. He then rolled one down the hill side and in amoung them it droped and exploded. They could not stand this, and the White Flag was hoisted immediately, And Lieut Col. and his party walked out as prisoners.

On Saturday things went on as usual, a continuous fire was kept up all day, in fact this is as regular as the rising and the setting of the Sun. And tho, I should not mention it to you, as a part of each days work, yet it goes on. You have not the fainest idea of what this Seige is. The suffering and deprivation of our troops is beyond description, and yet they meet it all bravely and patiently.

All every body you see is putting the question, "What is the News"? You would be amused and astonished too, if you could hear some of the Reports. Which are manufactured to order, and dis- upon the <u>Grapevine</u> now our only means of communication; but notwithstanding it has been cut and does not extend very far. Yet the part left us is very prolific and the fruit would do over justice, even to <u>Down East inginuity</u> or Yankee invention. You may be sure that a newspaper or letter would afford a feast of Reason and a flow of soul.

It is really a sad sight to see our poor horses and the public mules, going up, as the Boys term it. Many of them have been turned out of the lines to starve or draw Rations from the Yankees. The most of our Water is hauled from the river at night, and kept in barrels in the trenches. The cooking and Hospital camps are established in the Ravines between the hills or knobs for which this place is remarkable. The rations are here cooked by the men detaild as cooks and carried to the men in the trenches. The men in the trenches have a close time, I assure you, remaining at thier places day and night with thier accoutrements hung upon them all the, and if they look over the trenches, prehaps a dozen Balls salute his ears. up to this time the 40th has not had a man killed or wounded, In this respect she has been fortnate. The weather is hot and dry, had no rain here in a month. I see that the sick list is increasing. I must close.

Yours truly

No. 6
Beseiged Camp
Near Vicksburg, Miss
30th May 1863

My Dear Sir:
When I closed my last The Enemy was fireing upon our lines there has been no abatement, I think, the fire has rather increased. The Boa Constrictor is drawing his coils around us with all his strength. He has found that he cannot kill his victim at one stroke with his fangs, so he has concluded to crush us out by the Squeezing process. We have stood his <u>bite</u> and we will not be intimidated by his touch. Our men are determined to meet any

shock they may bring against them; and if human effort can hold them in check we will hold them at bay till the day of relief. On Wednesday night a party of several Companies of our Brigade was sent to the front to see what the Enemy was doing. This party was under the Comd of Col. [William Ezra] Curtis (41st Ga) He sent Capt. [Alex] Murchison and Co (K) 40th Ga. in front as skimishers. Capt M. soon found that he had flanked a party of the Enemy. - three or four Companies - He deployed and turned upon them and by his skill decieved them, and captured 109 of the Party. The others making thier escape. This was truly a success, even if it is on a small scale. Perhaps a party was never more completely picked up. They were led to Vicksburg, and thus thier guns are spiked for a while. Every little helps is an old adage. On Wednesday the 27th we witnessed one of the grandest and most terrific scenes that had taken place lately. About 9 oc.A.M. Three of thier Iron Clads From below began to steam up the River. When they reached the point opposite our fortifications, they then opened upon us. Broadside after Broadside and the fire from thier for Guns as are now poured upon us with all the fury that human skill can invent and power execute. The Boats moved up slowly, keeping up a continuous fire. It seemed to me that the thunder of Heaven had broken up from the Bowels of the Mistress of waters that even Jove had taken this as his time to deal out the bolts he has been forging for centuries past. The air was filled with thier shells and the fragments. In fact each and every place was filled with thier missiles. This continued for three long hours and one, unaccustomed to such, would have said that no living flesh could survive this fiery ordeal. But strange to say not a life or a limb was lost, except for a few mules. Surely an All-wise Providence protected us with his Shield. And did not allow a hair of our heads to be harmd.

When they came within Range ofur Batteri's paid thier respects in a becoming manner. After many rounds a shot from one of large Guns entered the side of one of the ugly monsters and tore off a large part of the other side iron and all. They took the hint and steamd down the River out of range of our guns. Where they have remained up to this time; and I presume will for a while at least. They never can pass up the River while our Guns remain on the bank to play upon them. And of this they are satisfied and know that it is worse than folly to attempt it. But thier purpose and mission on this occasion was not only to deal destruction and mete out consternation by whole sale to us poor Rebels, But a grand Fete, a glorious achievement, The best job of thier Brag Boat - The wonder of the age - The sum total of War Strokes - The final blow was to be struck and Vicksburg reduced, on this eventful day and there three twin sisters must join in the Melee of fuss and flames, and share the honor of the work, and witness the scene of the day.[23] The Cincinnati came down at the same time the others moved up But ere she got opposite the Brooke Gun above the city one of those kindred Bolts, that stayed the mad career of the prowd Keokuck at Charleston, passed through her and she turned and tried to make good her retreat, but the work was too well done. she got near the Bank above the City; and there she still lies to day, and will for many days to come. Thus resulted the charge upon the water side, which like those on land, terminated in one grand failure. At what point they will charge next I am unable to say. Many of our men are getting sick principly chills and fever. The 40th has about 80 on the sick list now. The weather is excessively hot and dry. A rain now would be welcomed by all. We now look to Joe Johnston. rumor says that he is getting a large force, and will in due time relieve us. Without hope the heart would break. We hope and we will hope until the last. And then if we are disappointed we must resign to the stern decree of Fate. We are sensible of the great and important issues now at stake upon the result of our defeat or success at this place. May God in his wisdom remember us in love. I will write you again soon.

Yours truly

R. S. Camp

No. 7
Besieged Camp near Vicksburg
Friday 5th June 1863

My Dear Sir:

One month has passed since I wrote you from Warrenton. I have tried to keep you posted with passing events here, as they have fallen under my observation. If you will not weary in reading I will not tire in writing, though I find this a bad place to write anything like a connected and Systematic letter.

The work of annoyance still goes on, and a few of our men are killed and wounded daily. But we thank God that it is no worse with us. My bussiness, as Inspector Genl gives me a good opportunity to learn something of the condition and will of our men. Our Men are confined to the trenches day and night. here they ly all the time exposed to the burning rays of the Sun, to say nothing of the exposure to the Enemy's fire; to all this they submit like Martyrs without complaint. I tell you these men will never be rewarded in proportion to thier suffering. They have stood now three long weeks like a wall of fire, between the City and the menacing foe. They deserve the highest mede of praise. You would wonder and behold if you could spend one day in our midst. We have been for some days past feasting upon <u>Pea</u> <u>Bread</u>. This is made of the meal of the stock pea, which is ground and issued to us. I can tell you that is is not very palatable, nor is it very sweet to the taste. Nor am I certain that it is the most wholesome, I have ever been a dear lover of Peas provided they are prepared in a certain manner or according to the old Constitution. But Pea Bread is a new dish. And we must practice upon it a while before we can truly say that we are fond of it. After is is cooked for hours, it still has a raw and indeticate [sic] flavor. I wish I could send you a loaf as a curiosity. To those of us who out live this war and get back home, we can then laugh and joke about the days of Pea Bread and Vicksburg. But we cannot now see the beauty of it. The fact is War looks much better when on paper than it does otherwise. I have before remarked that the Geological formation here is rather remarkable. It is one mass of little hills and knobs the sides of which are very steep with small Ravines or hollows between. I[n] these gorges, the noncombatants such as cooks, Teamsters, Qr. Masters and Commisaries, rendezvous for safety. You would be surprised to see the amount of labor they have spent on the improvement of the natural retreats. caves, caverns and dens are considered very fashionable and indeed, indispensable to good living and comfort now a days. These dens are of various shapes and all sizes. Some hardly large enough to shelter one man, others large enough for a family. some only a few feet deep, others going to a great depth into the hills. In fact I heard that a Surgeon in our Brigade had one 44 feet deep, and was not satisfied with that. If I start out to hunt a man I dont enquire for him, but simply ask where he has his hole or den; truly necesity is the mother of invention. As it is now time, and I smell its sickness, for Pea Bread, I must close. you know that eating, though a very ugly, yet it is a very important habit, and I have thought a very pleasant one, But the fact is he who waits to the second table here gets nothing, for as much as my mess hates pea bread, they leave no fragments to be taken up.

Yours truly
R.S. Camp

No. 8
Besieged Camp near Vicksburg
Wednesday 10th June 1863

My Dear Sir:

Since my last nothing new has turned up within the narrow confines of our Territory. The Yankees are determined to keep us awake, For small arms all day and artilery all night is thier Programe. But you would be surprised to see how indifferent our men are becoming to the noise, which is in verification of the old saying, that men can become accustomed to almost anything. To give you some idea of the extent of the firing of the Enemy, I will state the result or observations made frequently and at different times. I have often held my watch and never have counted less than one gun per Second within hearing. Now this is on the right of the fortifications or our end of the lines. The firing has been rather the heaviest on the left all the time. Now they begin with thier small arms at daylight or before 5 oclock and keep it up till dark or till after 7 oclock. But we will say fourteen hours incesent shooting each day. This reduced by the plain Rules of Arithmetic, gives us 1040 minutes or 62,400 Seconds, and now we know from repeated observations that thier shots will average two per second.[24] this will amount to 124,800 cartridges spent by them each day; now from this you can form some idea of the work going on here. And you may be assured that this is no exageration, these are plain facts which thousands will substantiate. The Enemy has not before laid Seige to any place since the War, And they are determind to show something becoming the Yankee character, and in keeping with thier boasted Military Prowess. Why all this

Shooting, when they know that they are doing comparatively no damage at all. They also know that they have us completely hemed in, and invested. And that there is no possible chance for us to escape. They also know that If we are not relieved by our friends outside that we must surrender and that this is only a question of time. We have just had a fine rain, which is a great blessing. The Branches had nearly run dry. The grass was parched up and consequently the stock is getting very poor. Many of them will die. The dust was intolerable, and the heat insufferable. Our sick list is on the increase. the 40th has about 100 on the sick report now. The exposure to the extreme heat, and the want of exercise, and the diet of Pea Bread all combine to make men sick. But with all this our men are in fine spirits, and hope is bright with them. All are looking to the day when Johnston will relieve us with fond and pleasing anticipation. I must close.

yours truly

R.S. Camp

No. 9

Invested Camp Near Vicksburg Miss.

Monday 15th May [sic. June] 1863

My Dear Sir:

Since my last the smoke and work of the Enemy has gone on, and our Boys has [sic] bravely stood thier ground, Met every shock, and like patriots, quietly submitted to every insult and hardship - even to the <u>Pea Bread</u> "hoping for a good time coming". There is so many things here, scenes constantly occurring that would interest and astound you. If you could witness them, and yet I find it a task to sift out and shape enough to make an interesting letter. Much that would rivit the attention of the citizen has become stale to the soldier and regarded by him as of little importance and heedlessly he regards it as a trivial affair, common to passing events. In my tour of Inspection this morning I visited the hospital or Convalescent Camps. From the trenches I up went the Branch about three hundred yards, Then turning into a little ravine. Pent up all around by steep hillocks, I found a lot of tents and shelters roofed with brush and cane.

Here ly the sick and wounded, and a sad place it it is. Here you see one scorched with a fever, and his cry is water! water!! Here is one shaking with Ague and his complaint is Cold! Cold!! Close by is another poor emaciated form, so feeble that he can hardly sit up: he has had a disease so long that it has become chronic. Medical means have faild. He has no little dainties and nourishments to suit his lost apetite. He can get no relief. He is in low spirits, and he lies here as a picture of dispair. Me thought, O' that I could do something to alleviate the suffering of these my comrades in arms. Without a great change, and that speedily, I know that soon death will terminate his afflictions, and his warfare on earth will end. How sad for a good man, and a faithful soldier, thus to pass away, and not a relative present, to bedew his brow with a tear of love, and to weep over him as he closes his eyes on time. A little further on, and I find a group of convalisents. These have been sick several days, but are not well but weak. Among them I hear a murmer and soon I find that the cause is that they do not get enough to eat. Or that they are censuring the steward for not giving them more. Of course I knew that thier greatest pain was hunger and that eating was, at this time, thier highest ambition. Here I now come to the Ward of the wounded. One I find who has had his arm broken and it has just been cut off. Another has shared the same fate with his leg. Another poor fellow has both arms shot all to pieces. Another an Arm and a leg. Here is one who has been struck in the head. A piece of the skull has been taken out, and here he lies with his brain exposed to the sight. Of the groans and sighs, the indices of the most excruciating pain, you will never form a correct idea until you visit a Hospital. I always leave a hospital with a strange compound of feelings and reflections. The deepest fountains of my sympathies are moved and I regret that I cannot ameliorate the sufferings of my fellow men. I think of the condition of the sick at home in times of peace and contrast the two. I think of the sad fate of those who linger and die of disease, instead of falling in battle on the field of Glory. I reflect upon the Welfare of the immortal soul. When I left I joined a party of four soldiers bearing a litter upon which they were bearing the remains of a fellow soldier to a place to bury him. He had his blanket folded around him, and no coffin or Box can be obtained to enclose the corpse. He is borne to a little Hill top, and a hole for a grave is there dug, in the greatest haste. His remains are laid in the Bottom and the Hole refilled. Not a word is said as low in the pit they cover him. Not a tear is shed, as from the spot they hasten. A Board with the name of the faithful friend is set at the head to mark the spot. In a few years the green grass will grow over his remains, and the tiller of the soil will unconsciously disturb the ashes of him who lost his life in Freedom's cause. There is nothing new and yet all is new. We still look for Johnston to relieve us tho. I dont think he has had time yet.

Yours truly

R. S. Camp

No. 10

Besieged Camp Near Vicksburg Miss.

20th June 1863

My Dear Sir:

We are still holding out against all the insults that Yankee inginuity can invent, and bring against us. All the infernal machines and engines of destruction, that human skill can devise are hurled in our midst. I have not attempted heretofore to describe the Bombardment because it is beyond my powers. A Dickens might touch it with his pen, and a Cruikshank with his pencil, and they would fall short. Even such Masters could after all thier powers, only approximate to the justice of such a subject. I mentioned to you that the Yankees had a heavy Mortar Battery on the Peninsula opposite the City. It is near three miles from the Town, but the timber having been cut down it is in plain view. They also have some heavy Guns in rear of the City in front of our fortifications. Day after day, and night after night, have they kept up this earthly thunder upon us. The scene surpasses the imagination in Terrific Grandure, and awful solemnity. At night we can see a flash - a large volume of flame - as if it bursted from the bosom of the River; out from this darts a small red fire - it mounts higher and higher and yet higher still, until at last it seems to be tangent to the blue vault of Heaven, and mingles with the lights of the Firmament. on it moves, like a meteor or a shooting Star. Tis now over the devoted city. And like a Fallen Angel, or a Satalite of Lucifer, it decends with increasing velosity. From where I am we

Now hear the Report, <u>BANG</u>, which makes the very earth tremble like the fabled volcanic eruptions, or the heaviest peels of thunder. About the same time the little red star-like fire flashes into flame.

The smoke floats on the air like a Balloon or thing of life. you hear the Bang - It has exploded. Then like the hum of heavy marching, or the sound of a Bevy of frightend partridges, the fragments fly in every direction dealing out Terror and destruction, regardless of Age, Sex, or Condition. Ere one has filled Its Mission, you see another "Mount the Skies" and ride the circuit of death. After this another and another for hours: for days: for weeks - for a month.. . .[25]

We stand all this without intimidation, in fact we have learned to laugh at thier fuss and folly. And willing that they may go on with thier expense and fun. These shells are 14 inches in diameter and at this rate, if placed in a line touching each other, the line would be more than a mile in length. Besides this the small or light-artilery, is constantly firing from all directions upon our front. The ground is litterly covered with Balls, Shells, and Fragments within our lines. It is astonishing how few have been hurt. Truly if this was all we could stand them for years. But Sickness is doing more to weaken us than all the Yankee contrivances. We have now a large sick list. But few serious cases. Yet it is sad to see our men stand to thier Posts day and night, for weeks, worn out and fatigued and worn out. Yet they are in fine spirits and full of hope. All believing that our day of deliverance is near at hand. We must necessarily have some killd and some wounded. Capt. [Thomas G.] Foster Co G.[26] was shot early yesterday morning by a Sharp shooter with a Rifle Ball. He was struck just under the left shoulder blade. The Surgeons have not succeeded in finding the Ball. The wound is bad, but not thought to be Serious. And I hope he will soon be up again. Joe Bogle and our other wounded Boys are doing well.[27]

Yours truly

R. S. Camp

No. 11
Besieged Camp near Vicksburg Miss.
Thursday 25th June 1863

My Dear Sir:

Since my last there has been but little change except that the Enemy has increased on the right of our lines, and particularly so with his artilery, and with shot and shell he has kept us warm, and closely confined to the trenches; but with all this, he has faild to intimidate, or frighten us in the least. Our men laugh at thier noise and missiles with impunity. With all this artilery work they have not hurt a man on the lines of our Brigade. It is truly marvelous. Indeed this is an evidence that truth is stranger than fiction. No one could witness the scene and credit the results unless it be those who are here, and see and know for themselves.

You may have a desire to know something of the forces within the lines of this circumvallated place. There are four divisions, Stevenson's, Forney's, Bowen's and Smith's. I believe that there are about 12 Brigades. The agregate sick well and wounded is about 30,000. But to day we have hardly half of this number fit for duty. Our sick list is very large and on the increase. Many of the man ly in the trenches who would be in bed if they were at home, and hundreds of the poor fellows who are at the hospitals barely able to be up would take thier arms and fly to the trenches, if an attack should be made. Never did men suffer as much, and at the same time evince a nobler spirit of patriotism, and a determination to hold out until the day of deliverance. Which is now beginning to be a serious question. I have before told you that our rations have been reduced. And in order that you may fully understand it I will state what is allowed to each man per day.

1/4 lb Flour
" " Bacon
1 1/2 oz Rice
" " Sugar
1/4 lb Peas

You will conclude that this would be rather a hard place for an Epicure, and a hell for a Gormandizer. And with those who live to eat, and consume, it is truly a trying time, and they resort to any means that will enable them to satisfy a craving desire or a stinted appetite. Crowfish are now regarded as the best of shell fish, and are sought after at any risk or price. Frogs are deemed a great delicacy and one dare not show his head above water, if he does the next leap lands him into the Mess kettle. Rats, which grow to full size in this Section, are hunted with as much eagerness as squirrels or Rabbits at home; and are eat with as much grace as poultry or pig. On yesterday I was invited to dine with a Mess of Convalescent Officers. They had Rats made into a chicken Pie, and the larger ones they had fried. It was very nice indeed; and the manner in which it was taken in proved that our prejudices often keep us from enjoying the Good things of life. I learn that some have been experimenting on Mule flesh, as Beef, and that it is pronounced not only good, but very good. In the War of the Revolution Gen. Marion and his men eat roots, In the Creek Indian War Jackson and his men eat Cow skins. I tell you there are men who can, and will, do all these things if necessary for the cause of the South.

We are well aware of the fact that to hold this place is one of the greatest importance to our cause. We know that if it fails, the war is prolonged for months, perhaps for years. We know that to hold it, and break the present foothold of the Enemy, that he is crippled, and his western Campaign a failure And that he will not "on to Vicksburg" for some time to come, and that he will be forced to give up the job in disgust and disgrace. I tell you, if we succeed here, and the Enemy is driven off, it will be the proudest day of the Confederacy. We believe that soon Johnston will in a few days attack Grant, and that when he does, he will defeat him. We know however, that Grant has a large force and that he has the best fighting troops in the Federal Army - The boasted heroes of Ft. Donelson and the Veterans of Shiloah. We know that Johnston must fight Grant upon his own ground. And that Grant is doubless strongly fortified in his position. With these facts then before us we know something in the work that Johnston has before him. - a Bloody task indeed - to accomplish which will require nerves of steel, and a spartan will. It will be one of the Bloodiest Episodes of the age, if the signs of the times portend truth, or "coming events cast thier shadows". All have the utmost confidence in Johnston and believe that he is the man for the emergency. That in due time he will route Grant and his Federal hords from the rear of

Vicksburg, and again we can breathe the free atmosphere and enjoy the inestimable blessing of hearing from our friends again, and know something of what is going on in the outer world. for sure we know but little now, having been pent up now 40 days. The 40th is still suffering with sickness, mostly chills. Since my last we have had several casualties in the Regt. On Monday the 22d inst Lieut A.N. Carter[28] Co. C was killed in the trenches. He was shot through the head with a mini Ball, and died instantly. He was an excellent young man, a gallant and faithful Officer. his place will be hard to fill in his company. On the same day Richard Hobbs Co. G was also killed. He was on picket, was shot through the head and died in about an hour. He never spoke after he was shot. He was a true and faithful soldier. On Saturday the 20th inst. A.C. Norton[29] Co. F was killed in the trenches. A mini ball entered the mouth, and he died instantly. He was a Non Comd Officer and as faithful as they are made. On Thursday the 25th, or to day [John H.] Lester Co. K, was shot through the head with a mini Ball and died instantly. He was at the cooking camp, Several hundred yards in rear of the trenches and was killed by a random shot from a sharpshooeter, at least 1000 or 1200 yards off. How sad and unexpected. No better soldier than Lester was in the Regt. Besides these killed we have had several wounded, none seriously however. Capt. Foster is getting on as well as could be expected. I fear that I tire you with my long letter. May Heavens Richest blessings rest upon us all, and guid us through these trying times, is the prayer of your Friend,

    R. S. Camp

No. 12
Besieged Camp
Near Vicksburg
30th day June 1863

    My Dear Sir:

    When we were boys, we to great pleasure in that good old game called Bull pen. But much of our pleasure arose from the alternate change of each side playing in the holes, our using the Ball. In this case the game is different. We have been in the pen now 46 days And the Feds have had the Moles, and have been "juggling and running down the lines", keeping the "Ball hot". all the time, you may rest assured that we would like to get out of the pen, and play on the lines a while.

It is also a game at chess, in which Grant has Pemberton in a close place, in fact he has had us in check so long that in may be termed a <u>Stale</u>mate. And unless Joe Johnston plays on his side of the Board, successfully and soon, we will be <u>swept off the Board</u>. We still hope that Gen. Joe will soon make a <u>ten strike</u> and give Pemberton a chance to <u>move</u> again.

Grant is still doing all in power to subjugate the place. He spares no pains that in his judgement will hasten the day that he can say Vicksburg has fallen. . . .[30]

For the last two or three days it has been more quiet than usual on the lines. I presume that they have at least learned by experience that the honor of breaking our lines is not in store for them, and that at last they have concluded to stand back and let starvation and want do a work that they have thus far, failed to accomplish. This does not say much for thier skill. . . .[31]

In my last I told you of the shortness of our Rations and that everything was now being used that will support life. And tho to you and many, my statements may seem to be exagerated, I here state to you that such is not the case. My object has been, all the time, to relate facts, and to this I will continue. I have no need to speak otherwise. for the facts occurring arround us daily are stranger than fiction. The question of subsistence is now a very serious one indeed. upon it depends greatly the fate of Vicksburg and the army within the lines. My fear is that the Rations will give out before Johnston can relieve us, and when they fail we can hold out no longer. It was said when the seige began that we could subsist on them 90 days. I doubted then. I doubt it still. My opinion is that what is done to save us must be done by the 15th of July, or else it will be too late.

We are willing to eat mules and horses, if it is necessary to save this place. . . .[32]

There is not yet a day but someone is killed at some point on the lines. As yet there has been but one Gen Officer killed and that was on last Saturday the 27th inst. . . .[33]

I had the pleasure of a personal acquaintence with Gen. Green, And can say that he was all and more too, that the above notice says of him.

The health of the 40th is still bad. Many of the men are suffering with chills and Fevers, and, sad to say, the medicine is nearly exhausted. It is a sad sight to see how badly many of our men look, and yet they stand to thier posts day and night. O that the day of relief would come, especially for those who have so nobly stood and suffered for more than six long weeks.

The only casualty in our Regt. since my last is by a wound by a fragment of a shell which Capt Murchison Co. K. received in the foot yesterday.[34] The shell struck on top of his foot, breaking two bones and leaders. It is not thought that it will endanger his foot. He will be laid up some time. Our wounded boys are getting on well.

I hope to see you face to face soon, when we can talk to our satisfaction. Yours truly

R. S. Camp

No. 13
Besieged Camp Near Vicksburg Miss.
Friday Night 3d July 1863

My Dear Sir:

In my last I told you of our exposed condition and unpleasant situation, which in the main has not changed for the better. The weather is oppressively hot, and from the long and exposed condition of our soldiers in the trenches, many of them are getting sick, and consequently in proportion as our ranks are thind, our lines are weakend. It is a sad fact but none the less true that we are daily growing weaker. And unless we soon get help from the outer world we must give it up - yield to the overwhelming force now against us - all our labor and suffering in vain and Vicksburg lost! Our soldiers have stood with strong arms and hopeful hearts like a wall of fire and repelled every onset of the Enemy, And have proudly anticipated the day when Gen. Johnston would come to the rescue; but hope defered maketh the heart sick, and disappointment will shake the firmness of the Brave. I think I see the indications in our midst of despondency. Too long have we been told that help was at hand. Hope, lost, and all is gone. Judging from the signs and developments of the last day or two. I opine that our rations are nearly out, And that Gen. P. will now fall back upon the <u>Dogma</u> of his <u>dog</u> Speach which he is said to have made some days ago, When Dogs and Mules would be resorted to for Rations before he would Surrender. The fact is the crisis has nearly come. The Commissaries have been killing and issuing Mules to day, and many of the soldiers have for the first time in life enjoyed a mule steak for supper. Not as a matter of choice but from stern necessity. There is no use to conceal the fact or hide the truth. Starvation is at the door, and what he cannot do any one knows. Grant may fail, in fact with all his skill and vaunted power, he has faild, But necessity is omnipotent, and must soon complete its work and then Grant may come in, and claim the honor and wear the Laurels. I have it from the Best Authority that some days ago Gen. P. had laid four days rations of Bacon and flour to use in case of an emergency. I presume the Emergency is that is Johnston should strike in the rear Then we might attempt to cooperate with him. Besides this, I know that our eating Dept. has nearly played out, unless it be a little Rice and sugar, which of itself is a very poor Bill of fare.

The enemy is still as determined as he can be, and has not relaxed in his efforts. By means of his approaches he has succeeded in reaching our works and mining them. On yesterday they blew up a very strong point on our left, several men of a Missouri Company were killed. But the others resisted the charge and the Yanks did not get in.[35] White Flags were raised to day about 10 oc. and the firing ceased on both sides and all this evening and up to this time everything is quiet. A calm reigns supreme. What this means I do not <u>now</u> know. Rumor says that a correspondence is going on between the Belligerants. I must in this case exercise patience, and let time develope the sequel. I know the truth will out and in this instance I know the suspense, though intolerable, will be short.

I know we are now on a turning point and though I still hope for the best yet, I can but think of the probable worst. I know that a few more days and the matter will be settled. Either Johnston must relieve this Garrison and thus save Vicksburg, or we must surrender and thus Grant takes Vicksburg, and a necessary consequence Opens the Mississippi River, and divides the Confederacy - But I will not now discuss the results of the fall of this place.

Should the worst come, I, with many others, will stand a good chance to spend the summer up North. If circumstances will permit, I will write you again as soon as I learn the object end result of the cessation of Hostilities. I will close, I hope to see you at some future day. then I can tell you all. Excuse this hasty scroll

As yours in suspence

R. S. Camp

No. 14

Surrendered Camp near Vicksburg Miss.

<u>Saturday night</u> "Fourth" July 1863

My Dear Sir:

I closed my letter last night in great suspense with a promise to post you, at the earliest convenience, as to the events which at that time were transpiring around us. our fate was then hung up in obscurity, and the signs of the times portended sad consequences for us in the mystic future. The dark veil has been raised - The mask thrown off and we are now permitted to glance at the destiny which the fortune of war has shaped and had in store for us. For the present doubts and hopes are banished, and we are the doomed creatures of a sad reality. We have been allowed to survive the varying vicissitudes of war and to behold the rising Sun of another <u>Fourth</u> of July. The boasted Aniversary of American Independence. The day upon which a noble, and Patriotic Band of our Ancestors <u>Declared</u> that an Infant Nation could and must be Free. The day upon which the <u>Sentiment</u> was spoken - The "Lute string of Liberty" was touched, it struck in unison upon the chords of millions of patriotic hearts its vibrations like a wave rolled on, permeating all the ramifications of a mixed and wild people, to the outpost and videttes of of a grand and wide domain. The reverberations then echoed back the response. <u>For this</u>, "We pledge our lives, our Fortunes, and our Sacred Honor". Not did it stop at this, But like an Electric shock it struck at the Throne of an Arrogant King and Corrupt Counsil who had with impunity <u>usurped</u> the <u>people's power</u>. Nor did it cease until this proud Despot "Acknowledged that Political power rested or is "based upon the consent of the governed". We have been taught to regard this day with the highest civil and patriotic Reverence.

Its return has been hailed with pride and festivity. Statesmen have on the return of this day met thier Fellow citizens "by thousands assembled" and expounded the beauty of our Republican Institutions, and pronounced with pathos & zeal, the highest enconiums upon the <u>founders</u>. The school Boy in his teens, in a Rustic grove poured out his soul in a Fourth of July Oration, to the admiration of the good people of the Rural district. The Demigogue has met the people in masse and harangued them upon the issues of some "deep and vital Political question". The gray haired Sire, and the beardless Boy, the Matron and the Maiden have all for near two ages consented and contributed to make this the Birth day of our once great Nation's Indepence a happy and joyous occasion. But alas! how changed The old Sage might well exclaim. "Alas! Alas!! My once happy but now ruined country. The noble work or a century torn down in a day." But I am digressing. And will write of the scene around me. All remained as calm as death during the night last night, And until 10 oc. to day. It was then announced in orders that the struggle was over, that the die was cast, The noble Garrison after a gallant defense of 49 days was surrendered. That Vicksburg was given up. It would be useless for me to attempt to describe the scene. Our brave men though worn out with fatigue and exposure had been cheerful up to this time, were now seized with gloom and despair. As they marched out in front of the trenches they had so long defended, and stacked thier arms, and upon them hung thier accoutrements, down many war worn cheeks did the Big and bitter tear run, and the deep tones came up in earnest accents, "<u>I would rather die in the trenches than submit to this</u>." The scene calls to my mind the time when the Hebrews "hung thier Harps upon the willows and wept". We staked our arms and colors about 11 oc. and the Yankees marched up immediately and took possession of the arms and the fortifications, we falling back and bivouaking in the Ravines. Gen. Grant and Staff entered Vicksburg at 10 oc. to day with all the pomp and pride of a conqueror. He doubtless feels that he is the Hero of the U.S. Army and I believe he is. His forces marched in and took possession of all the Ordnance and Ordnance stores with all the Batteris and Fortifications. I must however do them justice to say that they behaved better than I expected. They did not make any undue noise or demonstrations.

At 11 oc. the Boats below and the Fleet above the City, with all colors flying, moved to the Wharf. at the same time a Division marched into the City. When all had met, The national salute was fired. Of course it was a Glorious Fourth of July for the Union Army. and perhaps the proudest day of Grant's Life. And you may know it was a gloomy day for, or to us. Doubtless many of the Yanks thought of us as was said by one of old "Behold ye despisers and wonder and perish".

I am now prepared to say that my fears of spending the summer up north are removed. By the terms of the Surrender we are all to be Paroled. Officers are allowed to reteain thier side arms and private property (Negros excepted). These are the most liberal terms that any prisoners have obtained during this War. The Paroling Office will be opend to morrow, but it will take several days to parole the army. I hope it will be done at the earliest convenience, as I now desire to get away from this place as soon as possible. For I tell you our associations are not pleasant. In my last I told you that our provisions were nigh exhausted. Gen. Grant has ordered that our Army be fed from his supplies, which will begin tomorrow. You will hear much said in relation to our suffering here. There has been no actual suffering for the want of provision. A days Rations of Mule Beef was issued this morning to our Brigade, and many of our men have eat of it to day. I took a Mule Beef Steak for breakfast this morning. And I must say that it was very nice. Our prejudices have much to do with our eating. The long ears stood up in bold relief (Imagination) while feasting upon it.

You will hear various reports relative to the number of men surrendered here. I do not know how many have surrenderd to day, but I do know this fact, that not less than 31,000 have been drawing Rations during the seige. And the presumption is that about that number have surrendered. I am pretty well informed that not less than 5000 stands of arms, and large quantities of ammunition have gone into the hands of the Enemy. I do not know the number of pieces of Artilery that have been lost to us, But the loss is heavy and some of the best in the Confederacy has now changed hands.

This is not the proper time to speak freely of this sad reverse to our arms. A time will certainly come when this case will be investigated, and the <u>Guilt</u> or <u>neglect</u> ferretited [sic.] out. Every one is loud in censuring Gen. Pemberton. Some charge him as a traitor. others, for imbecility or incompetency. I think I have seen some evidence of the latter. But I will not say as much as I feel at this time.

I hope to be on the march in a few days towards a more congenial camp.

Yours truly.

R. S. Camp

No. 15

Paroled Camp Near Vicksburg Miss

Saturday Eveng 11th July 1863

My Dear Sir -

When I closed my last one week ago I then hoped and expected to have left this place before now. But here we are yet. Such a week of anguish and suspense I have never spent. And I hope never to have to spend such a time again. We have been surrounded and subject to the supreme contempt of the Yankees of [sic] Masters at present. And while they have in the main treated us very well Yet I am sick and disgusted with the close proximity to those for whom I have such low and degrading opinions. The very atmosphere is pregnant with a peculiar Malaria, Which is sickening to a Freeman, and not calculated to stimulate the drooping spirits of a War worn Rebel. It is true that we have met among our Conquerors some good Men And among them a few who still have a little of the milk of human kindness left in thier hearts. And personally I have received all that I could ask or wish at thier hands. And thier kindness I will never forget.

But in the present struggle we are Enemies, and must remain at dagger-points till this War is closed. There is no doubt in my mind that if this matter was left to the men who stand front in Battle and danger, they would settle it some way or other. The cause of our delay here is that none are allowed to leave until all are paroled. I was paroled last Sunday (the 5th inst) Enclosed I send you a copy of my Parole. This is rather a tight paper. Each soldier and Officer has been furnished with a copy. We get this in lieu of a passport up north. And I must say that I like it better. The business of Paroling was finished this evening. Our Soldiers have been going out all day to day. Our Division will start to morrow morning. the 40th will start at Sunrise. The sadest feature about it is the large number of our men we must leave behind, sick. In the 40th we will leave 120 and equally as many will start who will not be able to make the trip. I think we will have to march to some point on the Mobile & Ohio R.R. Well may we dread it. I will write you again.

Yours truly

R. S. Camp

No. 16
Camp Near Enterprise Miss
Monday 20th July 1863

My Dear Sir:

I wrote you last on the evening of the 11th inst. In which I stated that we would leave Vicksburg and all its associations, good and evil, on the next morning. And accordingly on Sunday morning the 12th July 1863 just eight long weeks after we had marched into the Hill City we passed the Yankee Guards at the Trenches on the Jackson Road. we were detain at this point about two hours. The Guards here examined our Paroles, and searched our Baggage to see if we had any thing <u>contraband</u>. We then moved on slowly and camped that night on the Bank of Big Black near the R.R. Bridges. From day to day we marched on making and [sic] average of about 16 miles per day. From Big Black Bridge we went to Raymond, thence to the celebrated Coopers Wells. from there a little place called Cats. At this point we left about one third of our men who had given out. from this place we went to Raliegh. There on to Garlandsville, and from there to this place, which we reached to day at 12 M. We left Vicksburg with near 200 men in our Regt. and reached this place with about 100. I turned and looked upon the poor worn-out and jaded little Band and wept as I said "These are they who have come up through great tribulation." It is really sad to look upon these all worn out with fatigue and sickness. And much sadder still to reflect upon the condition of our noble Regt. Those who were captured at Bakers

Creek are in a Northern prison, 120 prostrated at Vicksburg, more than than number strown on the wayside from Vicksburg to this place, partly within the Enemy's lines, and partly in a pine, Barren, and desolate country. When will we all get together again? I know It will be a long time before we can all get to gether, and our Regt. present a full and effecient organization as heretofore. In fact I know that many of the noble spirits will never meet again. Ere this sad reverse is over Many will have ceased to live - will have fought the last fight - and finished thier timely carreer. I think I have seen more suffering on this march than any one during the war. With our Misfortunes Heaven has smiled upon us. We have cloudy weather all the time and but little rain. Had we had a July sun all the time I do not know how we would have stood it.

We are now to be furloughed home for 30 days, and we will leave in a day or two for Georgia via Mobile. I will not write any more. I know you are tired of my letters. I have tried to keep you posted as to my movements and at the same time tried to furnish you with a detail of facts and events as they transpired around me. I know that my letters are very imperfect. For they have been writtn under very unfavorable circumstances. But they will give you some idea of the seige of Vicksburg and the part that the 40th Ga. Regt. played in that stirring Drama. For after all that may be said, It is one of the most important episodes of this War. And there is no doubt of the truth that you and no other person outside can ever form a correct opinion of the trials and sufferings of the Garrison who passed through that firey ordeal. Hoping that we will soon be exchanged and that our men will recruit in health and spirits and that we all will soon be at our posts in the field, when we can act our part again in the great and bloody struggle for our independence. I now bid you adieu. May the Spirit of the most high smile upon us and guide us in the Right and may our late Reverses be as a Refiners fire, and Fuller's soap to purify us, and cleanse us from our Sins, and lead us speedily to an honorable and permanent peace, is the earnest desire of your

Obt. Svt.

R. S. Camp

Notes

1. The only secondary account of the regiment is a short, privately published history, Dorthy Holland Herring *Company A of the Fortieth Georgia Regiment in Confederate Service.* Jonesboro, Ga., 198?).

2. William Stanley and Martha DuBose Hoole, *Historical Sketches of Barton's (Later Stovall's) Georgia Brigade, Army of Tennessee, C.S.A.. . .* [incl. Pvt. Joseph Bogle's *Some Recollections of the 40th Georgia Infantry, C.S.A., in Civil War* (Dalton, 1911)] (University, AL, 1984), pp. 6-7.

3. The following sketch of Raleigh Camp and his service is drawn from Camp's "The first campaign of the 40th Georgia"; Camp documents donated by his descendants to the Eleanor S. Brockenbrough Library, The Museum of the Confederacy; Lillian Henderson, *Roster of the Confederate Soldiers of Georgia 1861-1865*, vol. IV (State of Georgia, 1960), p. 341; and Robert Manson Myers, *The Children of Pride: A True Story of Georgia in the Civil War* (New Haven, 1972), pp. 1483, 1574.

4. See Bogle's accounts in Hoole, pp. 18-23.

5. *War of the Rebellion: Official Records of the Union and Confederate Armies*, 128 volumes (Washington, 1880-1900), series I, volume 38, part 3, p. 672; series I, volume 39, part 2, p. 854. Hereinafter cited as *OR*, series:volume:part, page(s).

6. James McPherson, *Why They Fought* (Baton Rouge, 1994).

7. The original transcription of Camp's handwritten paper was made by Museum volunteer Betsy Cole. Transcription and annotation for publication was done by Museum historian John Coski and Daniel F. Jasman, Jr., and Frank White, work-study students from Virginia Commonwealth University.

8. Col. Abda Johnson enlisted as captain of Company I on March 4, 1862 and was elected colonel on March 19th. Slightly wounded in action at Chickasaw Bluffs, Johnson nevertheless was titular regimental commander for the entire war. Henderson, *Roster*, p. 410.

9. Gray appears on Camp's list, but not in Lillian Henderson's published roster.

10. The only information in Henderson, *Roster*, p. 346, is that Gann was on a bounty roll dated March 27, 1862.

11. The 40th Georgia lost four men killed and 17 wounded in the battle. Confederate losses totalled 187; Federal forces lost 1,776. *OR*, I:17:1, pp. 625, 671.

12. Henderson's regiment, the 42nd Georgia, was in Gen. Stephen Lee's brigade, which apparently received more attention for its action in this battle than did Barton's brigade.

13. The 40th Georgia was not as slighted as Camp believed. Pemberton in his official report mentioned the regiment (as well as the 42nd and 52nd Georgia) as among those entitled to the "highest distinction" for their roles in the battle. In late April 1863, generals in the army discussed the proper name for battle honors to be placed upon flags ("Vicksburg," not "Chickasaw Bayou") and the regiments deserving the honors. The 40th was among the regiments listed, but it is not clear whether Gen. Barton issued orders to have the regiment's flag so inscribed. *OR*, I:17:1, pp. 669, 667-669, 675, 678.

14. This is a transcription of a copy of the order pasted onto Camp's manuscript page.

15. The remaining few pages of Camp's history of the regiment's first year described his duties on an examining boards for promotion and seniority, assessed the regiment's experiences and losses and mused at length on the prospects of peace and victory. "The Regiment has traveled about one thousand miles by Railroad, and has marched, on foot, much more. Our marching so much from place to place has given us the name of the running Regiment, or <u>Bartons foot cavalry</u>. It is true that we have not fought as many battles as many others. but it is no fault of ours. We may safely say that the 40th Ga has ever been on hand, ready and willing to do her part - to fight and die if necessary - and with as much truth we may promise that she will ever be ready to bear her share in the great conflict now on hand in which we are all mutually engaged in common cause for our just and equal Rights. . . ."

16. Capt. Joseph W. Anderson's Botetourt Artillery was one of the few Virginia units fighting in the western theater. As Camp reported, four of the battery's six guns were captured at Port Gibson. See Jerald H. Markham, *The Botetourt Artillery* (Lynchburg, 1986), pp. 25-48.

17. This landmark was the source of the battle's more familiar name, Champion's Hill.

18. General Barton reported (*OR*, I:24:2, p. 100) that Johnson was "sick and unable to command, but present and cheering his men.".

19. Harris was in fact killed in the battle.

20. Phillips was wounded several times and taken prisoner. He remained in Federal prison camp until exchanged in February 1865. Henderson, *Roster*, vol. 5, p. 448.

21. General Stevenson reported losing 11 full artillery pieces. *OR*, I:24:2, p. 99.

22. General Stevenson reported that Barton's brigade was entirely cut off

from the rest of the division. Barton said that the 40th, 41st and 43rd Georgia regiments acted "with impetuous gallantry," but were "terribly handled" when they found themselves cut off. *OR*, I:24:2, pp. 95, 100.

23. Camp pasted onto the manuscript page a clipping from the *Citizen* of June 13th describing the incident and reprinting a captured letter from a Federal sailor.

24. The former mathematics professor managed to calculate this incorrectly, as 14 hours equals 840 minutes and 50,400 seconds.

25. Camp pasted onto the page a clipping from the *Citizen* of June 18th describing the bombardment.

26. Foster was retired to the Invalid Corps, May 5, 1864 and assigned to command Georgia conscripts at the end of that month. Despite his wound, he lived to 1904. Henderson, *Roster*, p. 394.

27. On "the 22nd day of the siege" (about June 7th), Pvt. Joseph Bogle, of Company I, was shot just above his left elbow by a sharpshooter. The arm healed, but not straight enough for Bogle to handle a gun. He refused a discharge and returned to the army after an extended furlough. Captured near Atlanta in August 1864, Bogle spent nearly a year at Camp Chase, Ohio, regretting his decision to refuse a discharge. He survived the war and wrote one of the only published histories of the 40th Georgia. Bogle, *Historical Sketches*, pp. 16-17; Henderson, *Roster*, p. 411.

28. F A.M. Carter, listed in Henderson, *Roster*, p. 359, as killed in July 1863. Camp's roster also lists him as A.M. Carter.

29. "A.C. Norton" must be Cpl. William A. Norton, listed in Henderson, p. 390, as killed at Vicksburg, and listed in Camp's roster as W.N. Norton.

30. Camp enclosed a clipping, "The Grand Faux Pas," from the *Citizen* of June 27th.

31. Camp enclosed a clipping from that day's *Citizen*.

32. Camp enclosed another clipping from that day's *Citizen*.

33. The death of that officer, Brig. Gen. Martin Edward Green, of Missouri, is described in yet another clipping from the Citizen.

34. Capt. Alex Murchison survived his wound and was retired to the Invalid Corps in May 1864. Henderson, *Roster*, p. 417.

35. The Federals exploded mines under Confederate positions on June 25th and July 1st (not the 2nd as Camp wrote) and on both occasions failed to exploit the temporary gap created in the Confederate line. See Samuel Carter, III, *The Final Fortress: The Campaign for Vicksburg 1862-1863* (New York, 1980), pp. 281-287.

In the Field and on the Town
with the Washington Artillery

Selections from Documents in
The Museum of the Confederacy
Collections

The Battalion Washington Artillery of New Orleans was one of the most prestigious units in the Confederate army and has been one of the most studied regiments in the century since the war. *In Camp and Battle With the Washington Artillery*, written by the unit's adjutant, Lt. Col. William Miller Owen, occupies an honored place among regimental histories, both for its detail and readability. Pvt. Napier Bartlett wrote the equally acclaimed *A Soldier's Story of the War*[1]

Organized in 1838 as a local militia company, the Washington Artillery entered the Confederate army in 1861 and grew during the war from one battery to six, four of which served together under the command of Maj. (later colonel) James B. Walton as the Army of Northern Virginia's first artillery battalion. The unit survived the Reconstruction era as a fraternal organization, reemerged in the late 1870s as a militia unit and has served ever since as a unit in the U.S. National Guard. Throughout its life, the Washington Artillery has maintained a reputation for military efficiency as well as for social prominence. It is because of the conscious traditionalism of its members that the unit's history is so well documented.

While the voluminous records of the Washington Artillery were donated to the Confederate Memorial Hall (of which William Miller Owen was custodian) and are now in the Louisiana Historical Association collection in the care of the Howard-Tilton Memorial

Library of Tulane University, other important documents and personal papers were donated early in the twentieth century to the Confederate Museum in Richmond. Instrumental in building the Museum's collection was the Louisiana Room regent, Katie Walker Behan, whose husband, William J. Behan, had been a member of the Washington Artillery. Those papers include letters written by Capt. George Edward Apps and Cpl. Fred A. Brode to Brode's sister, Josephine Brode Trinchard, of New Orleans, the diaries of Capt. Edward Owen (brother of William Miller Owen) and Capt. (later Col.) John B. Richardson, a few other papers donated by Richardson, a memorial testament of Cpl. Frank Dunbar Ruggles and a handwritten copy of the farewell address delivered by Rev. B. M. Palmer to the men upon their departure from New Orleans.

Together these documents offer wide chronological range (from May 1861 until March 1865) and embody the diversity of a regiment's experiences. Richardson's diary is a dry daily record of his company's campaigns and battles from its entry into Confederate service through December 1862; Owen's diary includes many details on campaigns and on the logistical concerns of an artillery battalion, but is primarily the daily adventures of a cosmopolitan, rakish young soldier who moved in the highest circles of Southern society; the letters of Apps and Brode contain little detail on battles and campaigns, but are documents of daily life in camp, and offer insights into the peculiar anxieties of soldiers whose homes were behind enemy lines; Ruggles's letter to his father and Richardson's letter to the mother of M. Page Lapham speak to profound questions of life and death, loyalty and ideology, such as James McPherson explores in his ongoing study of *Why They Fought*[2]

Transcriptions of the Washington Artillery documents in The Museum of the Confederacy collections occupy several hundred typed pages. Selections from each of the document groups are transcribed here in chronological order, with minimal editing and annotation.

∼

I. Autographed copy of Address delivered by Dr. B. M. Palmer to the Washington Artillery from the steps of the City Hall, May 27, 1861—on the eve of their departure from New Orleans to the theatre of war in Virginia. (copy written February 28, 1893):

THE SOLDIERS OF COMPANIES 1-4, Battalion Washington Artillery prepared to leave for Virginia, wearing "their showy uniforms" and basking in the effusive adulation of New Orleans' people. William Miller Owen described the scene in his book,[3] but he did not publish the patriotic farewell address which Rev. B.M. Palmer delivered to the unit. In his address, Palmer offered an interpretation of the causes of the war and predicted the role that the Washington Artillery would play in it:

It is a war of defence against wicked and cruel aggression; a war of civilization against a ruthless barbarism, which would dishonor the dark ages; a war of religion against a blind and bloody fanaticism. It is a war for your homes and your firesides—for your wives and your children—for the land which the Lord has given us for a heritage. It is a war for the maintenance of the broadest principle for which a free people can contend—for the right of self-government. . . .

The theatre appointed for the struggle is the soil of Virginia, beneath the shadow of her worn Alleghanies [sic.] Virginia tried to be a buffer, but obeyed instincts to join the cause. Upon such a theatre, with such an issue pending before such a tribunal, we have no doubt of the part which will be assigned you to play; and when we hear the thunders of your cannon echoing from the mountain passes of Virginia, will understand that you mean, in the language of Cromwell at the battle of Drogheda, to 'cut this war to the heart.. . .'

It only remains, Soldiers, to invoke the blessing of Almighty God upon your honored flag. It waves in brave hands over the gallant defenders of a holy cause. It will be found in the thickest of the fight, and the principles which it represents you will defend to 'the last of your breath and of your blood.' May victory [illegible] upon its staff in the hour of battle—and peace, an honorable peace, be wrapped within its folds when you shall return. . . .

⁓

II. Pocket diary of Capt. John B. Richardson

DESTINED TO COMMAND THE BATTALION IN THE POSTWAR ERA

(1880-1896), Alabama native John B. Richardson joined the Washington Artillery in 1859 and was lieutenant of the 1st Company at the beginning of the war. He began his diary entries on May 25, 1861, the day the unit was mustered in Confederate service, and continued through the end of 1862.4 Richardson's brief daily entries were primarily details of weather, personnel changes and movements of the unit. On June 25, the battalion arrived at Manassas Junction, Virginia. Richardson made no entry in his diary from July 14-16.

Wed. July 17: left Camp Louisiana at 11 oclock and marched to union mills camped at night and left for Blackburn ford next morning

July 18: The Washington Artillery with 7 pieces was engaged with the enemy at Blackburns ford from 3 1/2 oclock to 5 Pm.— GW Muse killed—Wounded Viz. Capt. Eshleman J.A. Tarleton How and Tully. & H.L. Zeabul & Baker silenced the enemys battery and camped in the field

July 19: Encamped near the battle ground nothing of interest occurred during the night—rained nearly all night. no tents or fire.

July 20: Encamped at same place was paid off at Manassas from 26 May to 30th of June $116.66 bt WL Cabal [sic. Cabell] QM.

July 21: At 8 1/2 oclock this day was engaged with the enemy at Stony Bridge the battle lasting until 5 1/2 Oclock when the enemy was Completely routed. Sergt Reynolds killed Capt Payne was ___ _____ wounded.

July 22: Encamped near the battle field rained during the day and night which was very unpleasant no tents or anything to eat

July 23: Rained early in the day ordered to join Genl Earlys brigade 1 mile from Stone bridge. left at 1 oclock for that command arrived at 3 1/2 oclock

III. Letters of George Apps and Fred Brode to Josephine Trinchard, 1861-1862

GEORGE EDWARD ("ED" OR "NED") APPS AND FRED BRODE were friends together in pre-war New Orleans; both enlisted in the 4th Company, Washington Artillery, in May 1861, Apps as a sergeant and

Brode as a private, and both served in the company throughout the war. Apps rose to the rank of 1st lieutenant, Brode to corporal.[5] Most of the letters in the Museum collections were written to and saved by Brode's sister, Josephine Brode Trinchard, of New Orleans. She had married at the age of 16 just before the war to F. B. Trinchard. Although he did not join the Washington Artillery, Trinchard left Federal occupied New Orleans for Mobile, Alabama, in May 1862 to en-

J. B. Richardson
The Museum of the Confederacy

list in a Louisiana unit. In 1863, he joined Company E, 2nd Battalion Alabama Artillery, in which he served the remainder of the war.[6] The letters from Apps and Brode to Josephine Trinchard were concerned largely with their common network of friends, but offer insights and anecdotes about daily life in the Washington Artillery.

∽

George Edward Apps to F.B. Trinchard, Esqu., New Orleans
Camp "Orleans" Centerville Va September 2 1861

It is with pleasure that I address you these few lines at the same time I must excuse myself for not writing before, but I know that you will excuse me for the life of a Soldier is a very lazy life! the less a soldier has to do, the less he wants to do, but I know you will excuse me this time, and I promise not to be so negligent in future. Since my departure from New Orleans I have seen a good deal of hardship but I don't mind what I have passed, but I am thinking what I will do when the winter sets in. this is a very cold climate, and I am a very cold sort of a chap! So I don't think that I will like it mutch. But like or no like, I have to stand it. for the Washington Arty are "Regulars" of the confederate States, and as long as the war last they have to do as they are bid, and ask no questions. I like soldiering well enough with the exception of sleeping on cold ground in winter. that I cant go. we eat well, and are generally in good health, and besides the W.A. are the crack Battalion of the confederate army. and if we had a big name before we left New Orleans we have earned a mutch bigger Since we landed in Virginia. I think that Camp "Orleans" will be our headquarters until we are ready to march on Washington.[7] We have only three companies at this camp at present, the second being at Fairfax. there was a report in camp yesterday that they had a fight, but I dont know whether it is so or not, at all events the First, Third, and Fourth, companies and at this camp, we arrived here day before yesterday and have not quite fixed up; we have the prities camp you ever saw. It would make you wish you were a soldier to see it. Jeff Davis say's we are the model corp, and Major Walton wants us to keep up the reputation. I am at present acting Orderly

Sergeant I have a good tent and am quite comfortable I can get anything I want, such as coffee or sugar &c. Fred is with me, he is getting quite fat, you would scarcely know him. this morning he went after Beaver we having get our fresh meat.

We have just been mustered in again, and had a general inspection. We have received one month's wages and I assure you there is a good deal of Poker going on at present; some though cant play as they lost all their wages before it was due, so all they had to do was to receive it and pay out immediately. when I left N. Orleans I had $50.00 [illegible] when I have spent $150.00 and still have $23.00 left, so you know how I got it, my old luck of course. I want you to tell Charles that I received the box he sent me and the letter; but one bottle was broke, tell him it didnt make mutch difference though for we eat the contents. give him my respects and tell him I will answer when I receive his next letter. The weather here is bieutiful it is a little cool in the mornings but from 9, Oclock AM. it is delightful. we have very nice water here, and dont need any ice it is as cold as you want it all the time, and as clear as cristol.

The Seventh Louisiana Regiment is stationed next to us, and I meet a good many of our old acquaintances among them, especially in the continentals and Crescent Rifles. . . .[8]

⌒

GEO E. APPS

Lt. George Edward Apps to F.B. Trinchard
Camp "Benjamin" Fairfax Court House Va.
Sunday Oct 6th 1861

. . . Dear Friend I am very much greaved to hear that Joe Trinchard has done what you say. I told him when I left that he should not join my company for I knew he would not do for a soldier. He wanted to join the Washington Artillery but I persuaded him not too. I believe he has lost his situation by his joining the Orleans Cadets,[9] at least I understand Charles to say so, and that make me feel bad for him.

All the talk you hear about J.B. Walton you can tell Lucius is nothing but a lot of gamon, there is a few dissatisfied fellows in this Battalion, who because they cant have there own way, and do just as they like, think that Walton is not treating them right, but I think that Walton has done all in his power to please his men, and if he should resign his post, I should not stop here any longer if I possible could get off. he is the best officer that we could get, and to prove it he has been appointed chief in command of all the Artillery of the army of the Potomac.[10] We have all that we want in the way of eatables of the best kind and more than any other Regiment, we have fresh Beef every day, we have coffee and Sugar, Rice, fresh bread and in fact every thing we want, while other Regiments have to eat salt meat and hard crackers. . . . there is no fishing here, until we reach the Potomac river, probably I might catch some fish in it yet, for I think that we are about to have an other fight before long. it is reported that the yankee's are coming on us again, there is also a report that the Washington Artillery will be ordered back to New Orleans as the yankee's are sending a great many troops in that direction, but I dont credit half of the reports and I always wait for orders from head quarters before I believe any of these reports. We We had a grand Review here a few days ago, there was some 10,000 or 15,000 men on review, we had 12 pieces of our Battery in it, and it was a grand sight, you could look up the road as far as you could see, and there was glistening bayonets.. . . Ed

address my letters Sergeant Geo. E. Apps

THE BATTALION DID NOT REMAIN LONG IN "CAMP BENJAMIN," but moved back to Centreville, where it established "Camp Hollins" between Centreville and Bull Run on October 16th. According to the daily entries in J.B. Richardson's diary, the battalion's three months at Camp Hollins brought little excitement. Camped adjacent to army headquarters, the Washington Artillery received numerous visits from generals Beauregard, Johnston and Gustavus Woodson Smith. Richardson's comrade, Edward Owen, visited Richmond as often as he could get away. The battalion and the rest of the Army of the Potomac

George Edward Apps
The Museum of the Confederacy

were mustered for occasional special occasions, including the presentation of new battle flags (which Richardson described as representing "the southern cross") on October 28th, and the December 9, 1861 public execution of two soldier in the "Tiger Rifles" (1st Special Battalion Company B) accused of assaulting their officers. After a "pleasant" Christmas in camp, with "plentiful" eggnog, the men of the company were dispatched to begin cutting and hauling logs to construct winter quarters at a site near the Blackburn's Ford battlefield. By the time the winter camp, dubbed "Waltonville," was ready for occupation in late January, the weather had turned cold and wet.

∽

Fred Brode to Josephine Trinchard
On Picket near Fairfax Court House
December 15, 1861

I rec'd your letter dated Nov. 30th 1861, and was very glad to see that you and your family was well. I promised to write to you after the battle that was expected just about the time that you sent me your other letter, so as to give you the news about it, but that battle has not yet come off, but we still expect it to take place every day. We are all in good health here and ready to meet the enemy at any moment, and all our soldiers are as anxious as can be to have this next battle over, as it is thought that it will be a the grand battle. When we do fight the next battle it will be different from the battle of Manassas, for we have everything fixed up in style so as to give the "Yanks" a grand and warm reception. I d'ont think that we will be home by Christmas or New Years, as we expected on account of the enemy not advancing. Had they advanced, the thing would have been decided one way or the other (and we expect in our favor) and very probably we would have been home already, but as things are now, I c'ant tell when we will be home, as we have to stay here to watch their movements. But I hope it B will not be much longer before we will know. We have very fine weather here especially this last two weeks, it has been almost as warm as in September. Since winter has set it in, we have had a slight fall of snow, and a great many heavy frosts; but we get along very well. We have to do our own cooking now for about 2 months past and I have learned to cook almost anything. Our mess has a Splendid Coffee pot (but coffee is mighty scarce and dear) a frying pan, and a small <u>oven</u> or <u>skillet</u>, and I can make as nice biscuits as anybody. For this last 5 or 6 Sundays past we have had a nice Turkey, stuffed with oysters, for dinner baked in a stove. I think that is living mighty high for Soldiers. A turkey here costs from $1.25 to $2 and oysters 75¢ a quart and 50¢ for cooking it (which we have done by Beauregard's cook) alongside of whom we are camped. The only thing that I do not like about the cooking business is when my turn comes to wash the dishes, and that I don't like. We have no onions either to cook with here, we have got used to do without them and as for milk in coffee, I don't care for it any more. I get a quart every day, but drink my coffee without the milk. Sugar is scarce and dear also. it costs 25 [cents] per lb.

Your Brother
Fred A Brode

∿

Fred A. Brode to Josephine Trinchard
Camp Hollins, Centreville, Va
January 19th 1862

. . . Just tell [mother] that if I should ever be very sick or if anything should happen to me, I will let her know by Telegraph, and if I should not be able to do so myself, any of my mess mates will do so for me. But if I stay here very much longer I think you will hardly know me as the Country here agrees with me very well. . . . We have plenty of snow here, which makes the roads very muddy for us to walk to go and build our log houses and if it had not rained this morning I would not have been able to answer your letter as early. When we move into our log huts, which will be in two or three days, ~~providing~~ I will let you know how we get along. We are alongside of the Bull Run, and it freezes over and a great many of us have bought skates and are going to have some fun skating this winter. William Martin[11] is in our Company. About furloughs. If it had not been for the Burnside Expedition a great many of our boys would have gone home before this, but that ex-

Fred Brode
The Museum of the Confederacy

pedition has kept us back, even the Major himself cannot go, and he wants to go mighty bad, so as to see his family.

Your Brother

Fred Brode

Last night we heard fireing up to about 1 o'clock of heavy guns, over the Potomac I suppose that some vessels wanted to run the blockade and our guns fired at them.

∽

Lt. George Edward Apps to F.B. Trinchard
Winter Quarters Batt Washington Artillery
Blackburns Ford Bull Run Va.
"Waltonville" February 5th 1862

. . . The weather here is very changeable on the 2d it commenced at 5 oclock AM. to snow and it continued until night when it commenced raining and during the night it was so very cold that it freezed, in the morning when I got up the Icicles were hanging from the roofs of every house as thick as you can imagine, during the day of the 3d the Sun came out beuatiful, and it was quite warm, the snow melted and the roads got very muddy, yesterday itwas very cold and to day it is again warm. You will therefore see that the weather is very changeable, and in consequence the roads are very bad, in fact they are almost impasable, I therefore think that there is no chance of an engagement with the enemy possible before next spring on this line. We are now in our winter quarters and are about as comfortable as any one, are even at home our houses are built of logs and are 14 by 16 feet Each company has Eight houses, which devides the men so, that from seven to ten are in one house. The officers have a double house. that is two rooms for 4 officers my mess is a very nice one, we have one room for a bed room and the other for a mess room or parlor. our furniture has all been made to order and consists of a cubbord a table and some benches and a few camp stools. wse also have Two magnificent mantles pieces. The whole are made of imported (rose wood) in imitation of pine and if you <u>were not a</u>

<u>judge</u> you would take it for Rosewood. I tell you that we are living in style, and although there is not "Sams" here. I mean "Sams saloon" Still we have fresh oysters here when ever we feel like eating them, we have them in all styles, fried, stewed, and raw. we have Turkeys once and a while and other little delicacies ofthe Season, such as olives, pickles, and every morning we have a champagne cocktail before breakfast. wha do you think of that? but our champagne dont last long so we have to come down to whiskey cocktails as a substitute. I dont mean that I drink the whiskey cocktails; but I do the champagne. You will see by this letter that although I am away from home, still I am not so bad off as some poor devils are at home, and all I wish is that all my friends at home may get along as well as I do, And if i were certain that they were all happy why I would not care if h- freezes over. I hope that we will be able to whip the yankiees if they come at us, either here or in Kentucky or elsewhere, and that I may once more be amonst my friends, and if I am able to think I will have a gay old time. Give my best respects to Mr. & Mrs. Brode, Elison, Lena and all the children, also to Felix, Adolph, and all all the family kiss Josephine and Willy and receive the best wishes of your devoted friend Ed

Fred sends his respects

∾

ON APRIL 25, 1862, FAR FROM THE "SEAT OF WAR" IN VIRGINIA, occurred an event which changed radically the world of Ed Apps, Fred Brode and their compatriots. The Federal fleet under Adm. David G. Farragut, crippled the Confederate squadron in the lower Mississippi, ran past Forts Philip and Jackson and occupied New Orleans. For the remainder of the war, the Washington Artillery's home city was behind enemy lines.

IV. Pocket Diaries of John B. Richardson: Selected excerpts, June-September 1862

THE WASHINGTON ARTILLERY ABANDONED "WALTONVILLE" ON March 8, 1862 when Gen. George B. McClellan began his campaign on the Virginia Peninsula. J.B. Richardson's diary detailed the unit's movements during the subsequent six weeks from Manassas to Gordonsville to Culpeper Courthouse to Orange Courthouse ("Camp Taylor") to Louisa Courthouse into Richmond and, for two weeks, in the lines on the Peninsula. The Washington artillery saw no action on the Peninsula and moved back up toward Richmond, where it took up a position at Blakey's mill pond. There the unit remained until June 1st, the second day of the battle of Seven Pines. Richardson noted in his diary that at five o'clock that afternoon the unit was ordered to the front and arrived at seven o'clock. Falling back that night on the Williamsburg Road, the unit bivouacked for the next few weeks at the Garnett farm. Richardson noted that the Federals fired 162 artillery rounds from across the Chickahominy River on June 5th, made a "slight demonstration" on June 18th and shelled Confederate camps on June 23. The Washington Artillery, encamped at the Garnett farm, then at Blakely's mill pond, awaiting orders and assignment. On June 10, Richardson was promoted to captain and transferred to command of the battalion's 2nd Company. The company received an order to move on June 25th, but the order was countermanded. Richardson received a second order "to be ready to march at a moments notice Troops moveing during the night."

On June 26th, as the Army of Northern Virginia prepared to launch its attack against McClellan's army, the Washington Artillery was "ordered to march and left Camp at 6 oclock marched to the Mechanicsville Turnpike to wait further orders remained during the day." Though companies of the battalion were stationed along the Mechanicsville Turnpike, then along the Williamsburg and Darbytown roads, they saw little action in the Seven Days Battles.

With McClellan's army laying idle along the James River, the Washington Artillery settled into "Camp Longstreet" east of Richmond. Richardson visited the capital often in the middle of July. At the end of the month and the at the beginning of August, the Washington Artillery moved out eastward to confront Federal advances toward New Market and Malvern Hill. On August 10th, the Washington Artillery retraced the route it had taken in the spring, and marched back toward Manassas to confront Maj. Gen. John Pope's Army of Virginia. The march was often eventful.

August 19: Bivouac 6 miles from Rapidan River with Genl Toombs brigade orders to be ready to move at a moments notice. Marched at 7 oclock in the evening and Bivouac at 11 oclock in the Road. Genl Toombs was releived [sic] of command on the march by Col Benning. The command marched at 3 oclock in the morning and crossed the Rapidan at daylight. . .

Wed., August 20th: moved forward after 7 oclock in the direction of the Fredericksburg Road capturing Eight Yankeees marched all day in front of the brigade and just in the rear of the Generals [—] late in the evening one of the Gen's Couriers was captured disarmed and Shot by a body of Federal Cavalry near the ford over the Rapidan River Bivouac for the night and sent one Howitzer forward to support the pickets

August 21: ". . . we found that the <u>Spy</u> who passed through our picket had just been hung. met the 1st and 3d Companys at this point. moved on until we reached Stevensburg when we saw a man hung who <u>Deserted</u> from our Army at Harpers ferry. he was Captured in the Service of the Federal Army. . . "

Sunday, Aug. 24th: The enemy evacuated in front of the position occupied by us Yesterday. burnt the bridges over Rappahannock River and all the dwellings in the neighborhood. the rain of Yesterday evening caused the River to Rise so much as to prevent our forces from fording.

August 28: Marched from White Plains at 11 oclock and arrived at the Throughfare Gap late in the evening found the enemy in some force to dispute our passage. commenced skirmishing when the enemy opened on us with Artillery rakeing the Gap without doing much damage our forced pushed over the mountain and through the Gap takeing possession and holding it until after dark when the fireing ceased. Private Myers slightly wounded in the thumb. bivouac near the Gap.

Aug. 29: Marched from Throughfare Gap at 10 oclock at 3 / oclock the front of our column were skirmishing with the enemy also enemy artillery at long range about 4 oclock the engagement was general on our left. Genl Hoods troops being engaged until dark after that time our troops charged and took a Battery from the enemy

I moved down on the railroad with my Battery but did not have an opportunity of engaging the enemy

August 30th: Fireing herd all morning with Artillery at long range at 3 oclock in the evening heavy bodies of infantry moved forward and attacked the enemy and immediately the battle commenced along the entire line our battery moved forward and found the enemy giveing away and our troops rapidly pushing on found a position near [a] House and commenced fireing on the enemy when the battle was raging furiously. Private Henry was killed and private Blakely Ward and Summers wounded. remained on the field during the night and took possession of 4 new Napoleaon Guns Captured from the enemy. fired 143 rounds from our own guns 25 from captured Guns

Sunday, August 31: Bivuac on the Battle field and buried Private Henry White near the field at 10 oclock marched with my Battery and halted at Groveton found the Battalion headquarters and all the artillery of this corps of the Army ordered to report there at 3 oclock in the evening ordered to report back with my Battery to Genl Toombs brigade. marched late in the evening and found the brigade at Sudley's mills where we bivuac for the night

FOLLOWING THE SECOND BATTLE OF MANASSAS, the Washington Artillery continued its march north (along a route Richardson detailed in his diary) and crossed the Potomac River on September 6th. The unit marched as far as Hagerstown, Maryland (where, Richardson noted, the men were "very cordially received"), then, on September 14th, was ordered late in the day to Boonsboro to assist in checking the pursuit of McClellan's army. The unit "arrived at 10 pm to find enemy in possession of battlefield." On the morning of the 15th, the Confederate fell back to a position along Antietam Creek.

Tuesday, Sept. 16th: Remained in position in front of the stone bridge in Sight of the enemy, on the [left blank] River all day. some fireing at long range all day without any change in position. the enemy attacked in large force on our fron late in the evening. (all quiet at night)

Sept 17: This morning at daylight an engagement commenced all along the lines with Artillery which was kept up until 10 oclock when it became general on the left and continued furiously until evening when Genl Jackson turned their right and the fireing ceased in that direction. The Centre was hotly contested until 4 oclock in the evening when we held the field. on the right there was heavy artillery fireing kept up all day. late in the evening we were compelled to give up the bridge when the enemy threw a large force over the stream and attacked us furiously overpowering us with numbers and almost forced the position we however succeeded in repulsing them and pushing them back to the bridge Genl Hill's troops charging them just before dark at which time I was ordered to cease fireing. I fired from my Battery during the day's engagement about 350 rounds of ammunition changing position a number of times. I had in my company wounded Corp Hane Privates Fallon Freret and Brook (Aelewelt Killed) also Lieut John D. Britton wnded. This day at dark closed one of the longest and bloodiest Battles of the war rageing the entire day and closeing without much of an advantage being gained by either side—(lost 9 Horses in the engagement today)

V. Letter of Cpl. Frank Dunbar Ruggles to his father, October 22, 1862

FOR THE MUSEUM'S FOUNDERS THE SOLITARY LETTER FROM Frank Dunbar Ruggles in the Museum's collection represented a powerful testament to the nobility of the Confederate cause. The letter's donors had it bound into a slim volume also containing a printed "lineage"of Ruggles's family. Ruggles was born in Dorchester, Massachusetts, on August 7, 1837 and attended school in Boston. Only after graduation did Ruggles move south to New Orleans to go into business. In a short time he became a devoted southern patriot and enlisted in the Washington Artillery. Apparently estranged from his family, Ruggles wrote his father to explain why he supported the South and to assure him that he was alright.

∾

In the "Army of the Potomac"
Wednesday Oct. 22d, 1862.

Frank Dunbar Ruggles
The Museum of the Confederacy

To

Mr. Henry B. Ruggles,

Lawrence Wilde & Co. Boston, Mass.

Dear Father,

I avail myself today of an opportunity which presents itself, of communicating with you simply for the purpose of informing you of my good condition & whereabouts & thereby relieving you of that anxiety which a Father would naturally feel separated from his son by the irreparable breach which today divides & <u>eternally</u> separates your country from mine, & not with any intention of expatiating upon the merits and causes which have produced this separation. Alas! Who would have thought 10 years ago this once glorious Country could have been reduced to its present condition, who would have for a moment supposed that any subject of discussion however momentous could have been produced to the public mind that would cause men to take up Arms, Father against Son, & Brother against Brother, thereby forever severing the ties not only of friendship but of blood. Truly the people of the North are bereft of reason or a portion of them at least, of course I know nothing of your sentiments & even if I did should not allow it to interfere with my conduct or feelings toward you, whom I shall ever honor & respect as my parent, regardless of all National difficulties. Many doubtless with you are sincere in their belief in the righteousness of their Cause, but with <u>us</u> we are a <u>unit</u> in the firm conviction that our Cause is a just & holy one & "Thrice armed is he whose cause is just."

But in this I am overstepping the prescribed limits of my letter & must direct my thoughts to other subjects. Many opportunities have offer'd of communicating with you through returned & paroled prisoners but I have felt some delicacy in their violating the rules of War. I presume you have been aware of my enlisting in the Army, think I wrote you sometime before the commencement of hostilities that in event of its becoming necessary I should not hesitate to take up Arms in defense of our Rights.

I enlisted or Volunteered which ever one pleases to call it, in N. O. on 27th May 1861 & left immediately for the Seat of War in Va. with the "<u>Battalion of Washington Artillery</u>" Commanded by Major J.B. Walton, now a Colonel, & soon will be promoted to Brig. Genl. The Battalion is composed of 4 Companies in Va. the

1st Co. is commanded by Capt. C. W. Squires of which I am a member. The 5th Co. is in Ky. under Bragg, the 6th Co. remained in N.O. for home protection & was disbanded upon the disgraceful surrender of that beautiful City, to its present inhuman & beastly ruler "Butler". I have been in Ten different Engagements, including the Battle of "Bull Run", "Manassas", "Richmond", "Rappahannock Station", "Sudley" or "Manassas #2" & "Sharpsburg." In all of which the ["]protecting Hand of an Almighty <u>God</u>" has been stretched over me with but a single slight scratch, from the deadly missiles of an invading, treacherous & relentless foe. While my Companions have fallen on either side of me I have been preserved, Thanks to an Over-ruling Providence to Whose Wisdom & Care I commit myself in all future Efforts to defend our Soil & Maintain our Independence.

I am mustered in for the "War" be it long or short & although several opporunities have offered to become relieved of Military duties or to change my position from the field I refuse them all, & will continue so to do, I have enlisted for the War, & am determined to fight it out, so long as the present principles are maintained, My heart is in this Holy Cause, in this grand struggle for Independence & when it shall have been achieved none will retire to the peace & quiet of Home with a more firm Conviction of having done their whole duty to their God, their Country, their neighbor & themselves than I shall, and I look forward to a lifetime of happiness when the Independence of the Southern Confederates shall be achieved & God grant that day is not far distant in my daily prayer.

I am enjoying perfect health & only trust this may find you the same. We are sumptuously fed & comfortably clothed, notwithstanding reports in the Northern Journals to the contrary. I regret being obligated to go through a long tedious & active winter & only hope McClellan may be induced to advance upon us, think we are quite well prepared for him. I have sought among captured prisoners in vain for some person whom I knew or have heard of in the North, would like very much to converse with someone. I receive letters regularly from N.O. at last A/c G. W. D. & A.F.D. & families were quite well, of course much depressed mentally. Suppose the[y] will be compelled to take the "Oath of Allegiance to the U.S." but it will only be <u>forced</u> upon them. Any of my former friends and acquaintances that inquire after me please remember me to them as a "Rebel"

(As we are called).

Trusting and Praying that God may open the eyes of the blind families of the North

to a true view of their condition & intentions, that their ears may be opened to the popular Voice of the South which only asks of them the Rights, to be let alone & allowed to depart from a Union which is no longer a Union, in peace.

I remain your Son

Frank Dunbar Ruggles

Two months after he wrote this letter to his father, Frank Ruggles was dead, killed in battle at Fredericksburg on December 13, 1862. William Miller Owen recounted his death: "Corporal Ruggles, who, with sleeves rolled up, has been ramming his gun, suddenly throws up his hands and falls backwards with a ball in his spine." Ruggles, Owen noted, "had been cautioned about exposing himself so much while ramming his gun. He laughed and said, 'Oh! they can't hurt me. I've been here before.' The words were hardly spoken when he fell."[12]

The Massachusetts-born Ruggles was buried in Richmond's Hollywood Cemetery.

VI. The diary of Lt. Edward Owen, 1863-1864

As THE BATTALION'S FIRST WARTIME ADJUTANT, LATE WAR commander and postwar chronicler, William Miller Owen is much more familiar to Civil War historians than is his brother Edward. The sons of a tavern keeper, both Owen boys were born and educated in Cincinnati, Ohio. They arrived in Louisiana (the state of their mother's birth) in the late 1850s and entered the business and civic life of New Orleans.[13] Edward enlisted as a sergeant in 1st Company, Washington Artillery, in May 1861 and in September was promoted to lieutenant at the recommendation of President Davis for meritorious service in the Battle of Manassas. Wounded seriously at Sharpsburg and at Drewry's Bluff (May 16, 1864) and taken prisoner at Chancellorsville, Owen spent considerable time away from the unit, performing administrative duties and convalescing. Over 25 documents relating to Owen's Confederate service are in the Museum's collections. Among them are postwar reference letters from Col. James B. Walton, Gen. James Longstreet (Owen's postwar business partner) and Jefferson Davis. The former Confederate president testified to Owen's "high character as a gentleman and a Soldier. His correct and urbane demeanor, his zeal, intelligence and unselfish fidelity, conspicuous in the field and not less so in the day of his country's disaster, command alike my affection and esteem."[14] Indicative of his personal connections and the status of the Washington Artillery's officers, Owen was a frequent visitor to Davis's executive mansion during the war.

Owen recorded brief entries about his active social life, as well as details about battles, campaigns and the nuts and bolts of artillery service, in a pocket diary. The diary's sequence is confusing, as Owen mislabeled many January 1864 entries as January 1863. He began the diary on New Years Day, 1863, when he was in Montgomery, Alabama, recuperating from his Sharpsburg wound and continued entries until late January 1864. Written on the first pages are several lists: of the battalion's casualties at the battle of Chancellorsville; Confederate prisoners at Old Capitol Prison, Washington, D.C., in May 1863; and of artillery ranges and weights.

William Miller quoted only sparingly from his brother's diary in writing *In Camp and Battle*. Edward Owen published a brief reminiscence,[15] but did not publish his diary. Typical of most soldier diaries, the entries are brief and often cryptic. Reproduced here are entries which either provide details on the unit's activities or a unique window into the activities of a soldier about town.

> Thurs., Jan 1, 1863 Am enjoying myself. oh so much near Montgomery. Misses Maggie and Jennie H. I are spending Christmas week out here. Plenty of practical jokes &c. going on.[16]
>
> Jan. 15 Col. Walton, Miller, Joe Norcom[17] passed thro. Montg'y to day on their way to Mobile on recruiting service.
>
> Jan. 20 Left Montgomery for Mobile in charge of Misses "Tookie" Picket, Tollie Holt, Bec. Hales, and May Bellenger. Arrived in Mobile at 9 P.M. Met the Col. Miller , Mrss. Chaplain, Lovell, Story, Ethan, and Gr.
>
> January 30, 1863 Met Will Dudley in Mobile some time in the past week. Is looking very well. Is full surgn with rank of Major. Was asst. surgn to 2" Ky Regt. & after its capture at Fort

Donelson, went on Breckenridge's staff. Has now gone on Genl. Cosby's staff. Cosby commands a Brigade under Van Dorn.

Februrary 28, 1863 Left Mobile on Sta. St. Nicholas for Montgomery with Miller O. & Wade Smith. in charge of Misses Maggie Howell, Tollies Holt & Tookie Pickett.[18]

March 3 Arrived at Montgomery at 10 o'clock last night. Sent young ladies safely home this morning. Had a very pleasent & delightful trip.

March 4 My valise which I left at the exchange Hotel Mongt'y on going to Moblie. I found has been stolen during by absence. It contained all my Camp clothing. Serious loss these times when it cannot be replaced.

March 6 Dined with Mr. Jimmy Dick Hills who is now living at Montgomery.

March 15, 1863 Montgomery: To day Mr. Howell, Miss Maggie and Mrs. President Davis' father, died at Montgomery

On March 17th, Owen left Alabama to rejoin his unit near Fredericksburg, Virginia. Foul weather hampered what turned out to be a six-day journey.

March 23, 1863 Reached Richmond at 2 A.M. To day greatly to my surpris I met Morgan Harris. Came over from Maryland an Exchanged prisoner last Wednesday. Is going to join my company.[19]
Called on Mrs. Semmes[20] this evening.

OWEN SOON LEFT RICHMOND FOR THE CAMP OF THE Washington Artillery at Chesterfield Depot on the Richmond Fredericksburg and Potomac Railroad. His brother William also returned to the unit from recruiting duty in Alabama. Edward Owen made no entry in his diary between April 1st and April 30th.

April 30 Left our Camp about 8 A.M. in Caroline Co. Va near Chesterfield Depot for Fredericksburg. the enemy having crossed the Rappahannock near Deep Run on Tuesday in heavy force. Took 1 section of 1st Co. & of 3rd. 3 guns of each of 2d & 4th Cos. encamped at night. after a very hard days march near Jerrold's Mills. Left 6 guns of the Battalion in Camp, not having the horses for them. Raining & disagreeable when we started.

May 1 Started shortly after day, and halted at Mattaponax Church. Shortly after noon, went in Park about 6 miles from Fredericksburg. On yesterday the enemy moved up the River with his main force & crossed at United States & other Fords. to attack Genl Lee on his left flank, but Lee met them near Chancellorsville and held him in check. the troops with the exception of Early's Division & Hays & Barksdale Brigade went to the left. Heavy firing going on towards Chancellorsville nearly all day. Capt. Richardson with 2d Co. & Lt. Battles with 1 gun of 4th Co. were ordered off to Hamilton's Cross Roads.

May 2, 1863 Got orders about 8 or 9 o'clk A.M. to move to the front. Hear all placid in works on Marye's Heights opposite Falmouth. Large numbers of Yankees can be seen on the right. Some on this side of the river. About noon the 1st Corps D'Armie of Yanks moved past thro' Falmouth to reinforce hooker. leaving the 3rd & 8th Corps on our right. All very quiet in front of Fredericksburg. Heavy firing towards Chancellorsville. In evening the enemy on the right commenced pushing in our skirmishers & advancing on the Hills. We had no force to meet them. Genl Pendelton ordered us to leave our position & come to Telegraph road. Then ordered Col Walton to fall back or retreat to some safe place. Went about a mile when we met Barksdale returning. He ordered us back. Bivouacked in road all night. Early & Barksdale had started to reinforce Lee about 4 1/2 o'clk. P.M. Much excitement.

May 3, 1863[21] About 2 o'clk A.M. the 3rd Co. was ordered to take position on each side of Plank Road near Marye's House. Early in morning a Brigade of Yanks charged the Hill & were gallently reputerd by the 18th Miss. Col Griffen, behind the Stone Wall. About 8 o'clk A.M. our 1st Co. was ordered to Mary's Hill on right of the house when the 2nd gun came in to position the Yanks opened fire. The 1st shell went thro' Srgt. West's body & arms. The fire on us was very heavy & accurate. About 9 1/2 A.M. a flag of truce came out. About 10 the Yanks Sedgewick Corps suddenly charged our position. We had 2 guns of 1st Co. & 1 of 3rd Co. Blt & 2 of Parker's Battery & the 18th Miss about 350 strong. At the same time a very heavy body charged opposite Falmouth. We poured canister into them from our works & drove them back in great confusion when much to our astonishment we were fired on in the rear by the 6th Maine who had run over the infantry on our left in front of Marye's House came on our rear while we were busy with those in our front & took us at our position. Our last gun was fired when 6 or 8 Yanks were in the Entrance. It blew them to atoms. They also took Lt. Brown with the 2 guns of Parker's Battery & 1 gun of the 3rd, Capt. Miller succeeded in getting off 1 gun & the timber of the other gun. The enemy were very much frightened & excited when on Marye's Hill they fired on us after we surrendered Killing Corpl Lutman & wounding I.C. Florence severely in hip. They fired off their guns in the air &c. Wanted to turn our guns on Brown. Some one said that they were spiked & they left them alone. Were not spiked. We had ___ men captured & Capt. Squires, Lt. Galbraith, & myself. Capt. Everett flesh wound in the arms. Our Infantry was posted 4 paces apart behind the wall. On the left the 4th Co. lost 2 guns & the 2nd Co. 1 — Lt. DeRussy & Capts. Lewis & Many reported wounded. Our Caissons got off safely. We were taken to Genl. Patrick's Hd Qrs near Falmouth & paroled tho' we were still kept under a guard. Were treated very well and hospitably by Capts. Kimball and Cox of Patrick's Staff. Left on cars for Aquia Creek about 8 P.M. News from the left not good for the Yankees.

VII. J.B. Richardson's unpublished official report of the battle of Chancellorsville:

AT THE BATTLE OF FREDERICKSBURG IN DECEMBER, from his vantage point in the quiet center of the Confederate line, Capt. Richardson had enjoyed a "magnficent" view of the battle in front of Marye's Heights. Six months later Richardson and his 2nd Company found themselves defending those heights with less-than-magnificent results.

Edward Owen in old age
from *Confederate Veteran*

Camp. Battalion Washington Artillery
Near Fredericksburg Va. May 8th 63
Capt. B.F. Eshleman
Comdg. Battalion Washington Artillery

Sir I beg leave to hand you the following report. On Friday the 1st of May soon after arriving in bivouac near Fredericksburg I was ordered with a section of my Battery two Napoleon Guns under Lieut John D. Britton and a section of the 4th Company Lt. H. I. Battles two Napoleons to report to Col. Andrews Genl Early's Division at Hamilton's crossing which I did about 11 oclock the same night.

Next day all of Genl. Early's Division except Genl. Hayes

brigade was moved and my Battery was attached to his brigade. I remained in position near Hamilton's crossing until the morning of the 3d May when I found the enemy makeing the attack infront of Fredericksburg finding my Guns would not be wanted where they were I requested Genl. Early to allow me to move my Battery in the direction of Fredericksburg which I did by the telegraph road. when I arrived and found the enemy had taken Marye's heights and everything was falling back in confusion. I was ordered forward by Col Walton and took position in and to the right of the telegraph road commanding Marye's heights and immediately opened fire on the enemy who by this time had occupied the heights in considerable force. I fired from this position [   ] rounds of ammunition when I was compelled to fall back haveing no support and the enemy comeing up under cover of the hill so close as to force me to leave one of Lieut Battless napoleon guns his wheel driver haveing been wounded and one of his horses killed made it impossible to move the Gun in time.x {section in lighter ink added from below}

I have to report Private P. Von Colln and B.F. Kirk of the 2d Company wounded and Corpl J. B. Valentine and Privates Cary and Anderson of 4th Company wounded. The officers and men {inserted:cool} worked the guns well and acquitted themselves as they always do with credit.

Privates [Jules] Freret [H.M.] Payne [George] Humphrey and [John] Meux being under arrest were allowed to volunteer and assist in working the gun which they did to my entire satisfaction.x

xWe then fell back about one mile in the telegraph road when a new line of battle was formed. a Battery of the enemy made its appearance on which we opened fire and drove away. I remained in this position until late in the evening when I was relieved.

VIII. Edward Owen's diary (continued)

May 4, 1863 Reached Washington at day light. Were marched thro' the streets. then taken to Police station & huddled together till 11 A.M. were then brought out and found the street full of Soldiers drawn up on each side of the street facing inwards & across the rear formed 3's the soldiers closed in on us & we were marched to the Soldiers Rest. In evening the offi-

cers were taken to Old Capitol Prison & very well fixed. 6 of us
in a room with beds 329 of us in our crowd.

On this evening our forces drove Sedgewick back from the
Heights across the river with the loss of 5000 men. They lost
1000 when taking us yesterday. This their papers admit. Wrote
Miller.

May 5, 1863 Prisoners arriving state that Lee is still whipping
Hooker. We all in prison feel confident and cheerful.

May 6, 1863 Learn to day that about 1200 prisoners from the
Solier's Rest have been sent to Fort Delaware, amoung them
those of the "W.A.'s" capture. It now looks as if we were going
to have a big victory at Chancellorsville. Wrote to Mother.
Once in a while as the ladies ride past here they wave the Hdkfs
to us when the guard is not looking.

Every other day Dr. H.P. Johnston & Mr. McGann visit us to
take orders for any articles we may need. also bring us from the
ladies various articles of colthing &c.

Vallandingham was arrested to day on the 3rd by a U.S. force
at Dayton. Was taken from his bed at 2 A.M. Charged with violating one of Burnside's orders in a speech at Mt. Vernon, O.

With plenty of time on his hands, Owen made unusually long entries in his diary during his two weeks at Old Capitol Prison. (Excerpts
from those entries are published in Owen, *In Camp and Battle*, p. 229.)
He followed closely news reports and editorials regarding
Chancellorsville, Ulysses S. Grant's campaign in Mississippi and the trial
of Ohio's anti-war politician Clement Vallandingham. As early as May
15th, Owen expected to be exchanged and released, so his spirits did
not flag. Neither, it seems, did his engagement with the fairer sex.

May 17, 1863 Wrote to Fannie Millinberg in N.O. to day also Sam
Thomas
Only excitement to day in Prison is the expectation of leaving
tomorrow for Dixie.
Amused myself this morning looking at the ladies. The day is
very windy & as they pass they of course show their feet. And all
of them are large. have not seen a pretty foot yet in this city.
The wind blew the dress of a lady on horseback nearly over
head & the poor woman could not get it down again for some

time. showed her <u>spindles</u>

May 18, 1863 Did not get off today as expected for Dixie. . . . Number of ladies passed the prison today & kissed their hands to us.

May 19, 1863 . . . A big procession of Negroes marched by our prison with Drum and Fife. The white Yank heartily disgusted. A young lady passing the prison at the time called out "Why don't you hiss them?" and indeed we did. They get their arms tomorrow.

May 20, 1863 Left the Old Capitol Prison at about 10 o'clock A.M. bound for Dixie land. Marchd thro' the streets under a heavy guard to the "Str. sights of Maine" about 300 all told. One half citizens. Left the wharf about 11 1/2 A.M. and a happy set we were too. During the afternoon passed Fort Washington, Alexandria, Mt. Vernon, Acquia Creek, Occoquan, Dumfries, &c. Saw some very heavy fortifications on almost every hill below Washington also on Arlington Heights. . . .

May 21, 1863 Arrived at City Point at 7 1/2 o'clock P.M. Passed Harrison's Ldg. before dark.

May 22, 1863 How glad we all are to tread once more the sod of our fair Dixie land. to be free once more from the prisons of the North.

May 23, 1863 Left Petersburg at 5 o'clk A.M. & arrived in Richmond at 7 1/2 A.M. Find the city very dull and hot.

OWEN WASTED NOT A MOMENT IN RETURNING TO THE SOCIAL circles of Richmond. He learned through Capt. Raphael Semmes's wife, Anne (recently ordered out of Ohio by the Federal army), that "the Cincinnatians are very bitter against Miller & myself. Threaten to kill &c. us." For a week, Owen "loafed about town," calling on Mrs. Davis at the executive mansion, Mrs. Thomas J. Semmes, meeting the president and "a number of pretty ladies." Eagerly awaiting the arrival of Maggie Howell, Owen "had a very pleasant visit" with her on May 28th, then rejoined his unit on the following day.

May 30, 1863

Everything goes on quietly in Camp. It is a very pretty place on the edge of woods on Mrs. Stannards Farm in Spottsylvania Co.

& on the River Po.

May 31, 1863 Wrote to T. to day. the only thing of interest during the day.

The balance of our men that were captured are beginning to arrive in camp.

June 3, 1863 Recd orders for Battn to leave in morning for Culpepper C.H.

June 4, 1863 Marched this morning at about 8 on out Summer's Campaign. Went about 14 miles & halted at 3 P.M. for the night.

June 5, 1863 Started about 6 A.M. for Raccoon's Ford on the Rapidan River. reached at about 2 P.M. & went in camp on the North Side for the night.

Horses reduced to 5 lbs corn a day. & no hay. so have to stop early to let them graze.

June 6, 1863 Started about 7 A.M. & reached Culpepper C.H. about 10 A.M. Remained waiting 4 hours for Major Eshleman to find a camp. finally parked about 1 mile from town. Rained in afternoon.

Genl. Stuart has all his cavalry concentrated here. about 12,000 strong. Had a grand review yesterday, This evening they all took up camp and marched off towards Brandy.

June 7, 1863 Went in town & the first person almost I saw was Miss Nettie Gamis. Looked very well indeed. Promised to call on her during the morning. Went then to Genl. Longstreets. Ewells Corps passing this town. Saw Will Holt, Lea Bakemill & Lt. Col. Forsyth, & Genl. Fitz Hugh Lee [sic]. Stopped at Miss Nettie's about 2 1/2 o'clk. made us stay to dinner. very acceptable indeed greens, peas &c.

Genl. Lee arrived this morning. Learn the Yanks 10,000 strong crossed at Deep Run Below Fredericksburg and A.P. Hill has pitched into them and driven them across the river.

Have all kinds of rumors today that Kirby Smith has whipped Banks at Port Hudson & Banks lost an arm. & Grant in retreating from Vicksburg & Johnston is after him.

June 8 Longstreet's and Ewell's Corps are now encamped around Culpepper C.H. Some grand movement is about taking place. but no one can determine what it is to be. Have various rumors about the Yankees retreating &c.

Saml. Holt called on me this morning. just from home & gave me a very pretty Tobacco bag & pictures.

June 9 The first sound that saluted my ears on awakening this morning was reports of cannon in the distance. It seems that during the night the Yankee Cavalry crossed the Rappahannock at Brandy Ford and at day light attacked our Cavalry. Our Forces were surprised & a good many captured, but rallied and drove back the enemy. The 2n S.Ca. & 4th Va were the regiments surprised. The fight lasted all day from Brandy Station to Beverly Ford. Loss on both sides very heavy. The whole army here. Longstreet's and Ewells Corps. were moved from their camps. One Battn moved to Longstreet's Hd Qrs. Early's Division moved towards the fight. Early in the morning, a portion of Yankee Cavalry charged thro'. Slivens Fg to within 3/4 of a mile of Longstreet's Hd Qrs.

At dark retd to our old Camps. Dined today at Miss Nettie's & had Ice Cream there in the evening.

June 10, 1863 Started this morning at 6 o'clk with Lt. Battles for the Battle field. Met Genl Stuart there & rode over the field with him. saw about 50 dead Yanks amoung them 2 Cols. Went down to Beverly Ford & picked strawberries on full view of Yankee pickets. Saw our old Battle field of Rappahannock Station & the graves of our men killed there Aug. 23, '62. were in good condition.

Got home about 4 P.M.

June 11, 1863 Ewell's Corps left last night & this morning on the Sperryville road with 8 days rations on some flanking expedition.

June 14, 1863 Yesterday evening & to day Ewell's Corps has been fighting Milroy at Winchester.

June 15, 1863 Left Camp at 3 P.M. to day en route for Winchester. Weather very hot. March very severe on our new recruits. Bivouacked near Woodville about 12 miles march.

Before leaving called on Miss Nettie. Saml Holt coming out.

June 16, 1863 Started at 5 1/2 A.M. Marched till 11 1/2 A.M. & halted from now. came 17 miles. Started again at 3 P.M. & halted at 6 near Flint Hill. 6 miles. Making 23 miles to day.

June 17, 1863 Started at 6 A.M. & marched till 2 P.M. & halted for the night near the Shenandoah River. 5 miles from Front

Royal. made 17 miles to day. Are now bound for Berryville instead of Winchester.

Learn that Ewell has driven Milroy before him capturing (Owen Blank) men & (Same) cannon, (Once More) horses & large amts of munitions. That he has the Potomac picketed & has Martinsburg. Magnificent opening of the Summer's Campaign.

June 18, 1863 Started at 6 A.M. and reached Millwood at about 11 A.M. where we were ordered to park to await further orders. Have the news that Rodes is in Hagerstown Md & Jenkins Brigade of Cavalry is in Chambersburg, Pa.

Charles Thompson, captain of the La Guard Artillery was killed in the Battle at Winchester.

Made 10 miles today.

June 19, 1863 Still in camp near Millwood. To day about 225 prisoners passed here taken by Stuart near Aldie & Middleburg. Among them one of Hooker's Staff Officers with important dispatches to Genl. Pleasanton. Hooker crossed the Potomac at White's Ford yesterday & has left a large force behind to try & get in the Valley. but Longstreet's Corp is at Snicker's & Ashby's Gaps watching them.

Yankee papers say that Johnston & Pemberton are driving Grant before them at Vicksburg. Also say that our Cavalry is in Harrisburg, Pa & that the Pa Dutchmen refuse to respond to call of Gov. Carlisle for 100,000 more troops.

Rained like blazes to day. Could not sleep in our tent.

June 20, 1863 Still at this place. A.P. Hill coming up to day. Hd Qrs. at White Post.

Dark & gloomy day.

June 21, 1863 Big Cavalry fight near Ashby Gap. Yankees rather got the better of Stuart.

June 24, 1863 Orders came yesterday to move to Hagerstown Md. Left Camp at 2 1/2 o'clk A.M. reached Winchester at 7 1/2 o'clkA.M. 10 miles. Called on Miss Josephine Carson and Miss Hattie Hammond where we had breakfast. Reached Bunker Hill at 1 o'clk P.M. & parked for the night. Marched 23 miles during the day.

June 25 Left Camp at 4 A.M. marched about 2 miles when we had to halt to allow Picketts division to take the front "Here our troubles commence." [Brown written in between the lines] had to follow the wagon trains of the division. Reached Martinsburg about 12 M. Saw a few Secesh ladies waving their Hdks & c.

Crossed the Potomac at Williamsport at 6 P.M. in the rain.

Met with a porr reception in W-t. Our men went thro. singing various popular songs & in fine spirits.

Camped about 1 mile from town. Marched 23 miles to day.

June 26, 1863 Reville at 3 A.M. Moved at 5 1/2 A.M. The Battn had to wait till Pickett moved on. Then the corps had to wait till A.P. Hill passed thro' Hagerstown. Eshleman & I rode on to town. Called on Mr. Hagar & got to a good breakfast. also on the Misses Hurley, Doyle, Spangler, &c. Had a very pleasant time. Left town after 4 P.M. expecting to find the Battn 1/2 miles from town, but found they had marched on. Passed the Pennsylvania line about 6 P.M. & caught up with the Battn about 7 P.M. Bivouacked at Greencastle at 7 1/2 P.M. Marched 15 miles to day. Greencastle is 8 miles from Hagerstown & 5 from the line. This is strong Union hole.

Raining all day.

June 27, 1863 Marched this morning about 9 A.M. passed thro' Greencastle. Shortly after starting, I went off with Joe Wood, QR Ms. & about 10 others on a search for Horses to confiscate them for Army use. Rode thro' all the country roads for about 25 miles but found none at any of the farm houses. Ewell's Corps took nearly everything on his way up thro' here & the balance have been run off to the mountains. Joined the Battn at Chambersburg. Encamped about 2 miles north of the town. Marched 15 miles to day.

The Country people are very much frightened & are glad to escape only with the loss of their stock. Expected we would burn their houses, barns, &c.

Genl. Lee's orders are very strict about private property.

June 28, 1863 Rode to town this morning, but found no stores open. So could buy nothing. Genl. Longstreet has made requisition on the Mayor for 60,000 rations & if they are not funished promptly will seize them in the stores.

It is amusing to see the Union people turn up their precious noses at us as we ride past. Some of the ladies wear a small U.S.

flag on their hats & breast. The men look very sour & cross. We can afford to laugh at them.

Our men are delighted at being here and are very anxious to practice retaliation on this country for the wrongs committed in the South, but Genl. Lee's orders are very stricts & severe on that subject. As yet no damage has been done to private property . . .

We live finely here.

June 29, 1863 Still in camp near Chambersburg. We cannot as yet form any conjecture as to our future movement. Longstreet's Hd Qrs are on the Gettysburg & Baltimore road. but we on the Harrisburg road. Our next days march will probably show us. We may be waiting for Hooker to come up. & while our men are resting & fresh pitch into him and give him a good thrashing.

Left Chambersburg at 10 A.M. on the road to Baltimore. Stopped at Greenwood, 9 miles travel.

To day I rode out to the mountains (Cumberland) in search of a horse. found none. Rode 30 miles to day.

July 1, 1863 Learn that A.P. Hill met the Yanks to day near Gettysburg & drove them nearly 3 miles. Bivouac still at Greenwood.

During the fight yesterday to day Ewell with Early's Division came down on the enemy's flank from York & drove them like sheep. captured about 5000 men. A.P. Hill took about 1000. Genl Archer was taken prisoner. Genl. Heth slightly wounded.

July 2, 1863 Left our bivouac at Greenwood this morning at 2 1/2 o'clock & reached the battle field near Gettysburg at 9 A.M. Went in park.

Yanks occupy some hills just beyond the town. which they have fortified and lined with Artillery. 'tis a very strong position. Went to the front this morning. A.P. Hill's Corps. occupies the center. Longstreet the right & Ewell the left. formed |_| We have a great many pieces of Artillery in position. At 4 o'clock P.M. as Longstreet was going into position on the right the enemy opened on him. Our side replied & the battle was begun. I was on the right in front at the time.

Longstreet drove them about 1/2 mile very hard fight. The

Cannonading was terrific being Salvos. I viewed the fight from Genl. Lee's Hill.

Our Battalion ordered into position about dark.

July 3, 1863

At day Light our Battalions opened on the Yanks. & had very sharp fight for about an hour. had 1 man killed & 4 Wd. all quiet the balance of the morning expecting occasional firing of Artillery. At 25 min. to 2 o'clock a roar of Artillery burst forth and the battle was opened for to day. The Cannonading is truly lively terrific. On the right Longstreet charged the heights & fortications but the support not coming up in time had to fall back. The fight was kept up till evening with no advantage on either side. At dark we fell back to our original lines.

July 4, 1863 All quiet along the lines with the exception of the skirmishers. About 10 o'clk our Battalion was ordered to report to Genl Imboden at Cashtown ordered back to assist in guarding an immense wagon train of our wounded. Marched all day & all night very tired Learn that Col Griffen 18 Miss is Wd & Lt. Col. Luce is Wd & again a prisoner. Genls Barks dale & Garnett are killed. Lt. Col. of 8 La is killed.

Enemy did not fire a National Salute. During the day they shewed themselves opposite our right, but Hood drove them back.

Their position is too strong for us to attempt to assault again. Our loss is 10,000 killed wd & missing.

July 5, 1863 Marching marching all night & all day. Very monotonous. Raining too. This afternoon about 200 Yankee Cavalry charged on our train just in front of our guns. We came in position but had no chance to fire. Our Cavalry finally charged them & a squad of Infantry came up & drove the Yanks back. Killed one man & captured several. We lost 1 Captain killed. The Yanks only cut the spokes of 2 or 3 wagons.

[different hand] Nothing to be seen of Yanks at Gettysburg. have fallen back to Westminster Our forces left their positions at 9 o'clk last night. & marched towards Fairfield 24 miles from Hagarstown.

July 6, 1863 Reached Williamsport at 2 o'clk A.M. & were at once put in position. 1 & 2 Co's on the Hagarstown road & 3 & 4th on the Boonsboro road. Expect the Yanks by daylight. Quiet all day. Towards evening the Yanks made their attack on our right. They had a Division of Cavalry & several batteries of Artillery. We fought mostly all with Artillery. together with skirishing on front. No Cavalry charges. At dark the enemy retired. Col Kilpatrick commanded Yanks. The 2 Co. W.A. lost 15 killed and wd, 13 on one piece & 8 Horses, 4" Co. lost 3 Horses. Yankee loss heavy.

Genl. FitzHugh Lee arrived to night.

We marched continually from Gettysburg to this point without stopping for rest or to feed our horses or men. Marched 50 miles in 40 hours. Very hard.

Rcd letter from T.

July 7, 1863 To day all quiet. Yanks reported in front still tho' it turns out they are only stragglers. Some of our men captured some this morning & br't them into camp Horses & all.

This evening the Battn recd orders to cross the Potomac to go to Winchester with the train of wd, on the river bank one thousand of wagons collected & they have commenced crossing them one at a time on a Ferry flat. During the night the rope brke & so the crossing is stopped.

I stayed all night with Capt. Will Allen on this side. Battn is on the other. Our wagons & most of our men are still on this side.

July 8, 1863 Learned this morning that Genl. Longstreet's Hd Qrs. was on the Hagarstown road about 2 miles from Williamsport. Went out to see Miller.

Genl. Lee & the army have fallen back to Hagarstown there to refresh his men, get ammunition items & await the enemy if he comes. If not Lee will hunt him up. Orders have been issued to prepare for another action.

Potomac still so swollen from the late heavy rains that our wagons cannot cross.

July 9, 1863 All quiet. The Qr Mss. are busy ferrying the wagons across the river. tis very slow work

July 14, 1863 This morning the whole army crossed the Potomac on the Pontoons into Dixie. It is in good condition. Genl. Pettigrew was killed by some Cavalry of the enemy charging his Brigade & firing shot him. He was with Genrls A.P. Hill & Heth. Miss Tookie Pickett married today.

July 15, 1863 Moved this morning from 2 mile this side of

Martinsburg to Bunker Hill & camped. I then rode on to
Winchester. Staying with 3rd Co. now camped near here. Learn
the fall of Vicksburg is confirmed. 'tis a terrible loss to us &
causes the greatest rejoicing in the North.

Rec'd letter from T.

July 16, 1863 Have the news to day from the N.O. papers that
Port Hudson had surrendered. Misfortunes never come singly.
Got note from Miller this evening says Mr. Chaplain is so weak
he may die in a week. Will bring him to Winchester. Says also
the Army will move to marrow. Think Lee is going again into
Maryland.

Yanks are not quite so jubilant as they were a week ago.

Wrote T.

July 17 Found a place in town for Mr. Chaplain & then rode for
Camp. Met Miller & Drew bringing him in. very much shocked
at the great change since I saw him last. Is amaciated [sic emci-
ated] & so weak he has to be carried. Put him to bed. Tife
Wilking will remain with him & his boy, John. Miller, Drew &
myself stayed all night at Carsons.

The Army is still encamped around Bunker Hill. Everything
quiet.

July 18 Chaplain still very weak & tired from his long ride from
Camp, 12 miles, Breath very short. Wrote down his last
requests this morning. He seems perfectly resigned to his fate.
Does not expect to live more than a couple of days. He never
complains or grumbles. Eats very little or nothing. I got permission to day to remain with him during his illness. During
this evening, he was quite feverish.

Army still quiet.

July 19, 1863 Chaplain slept a little during the night & so feels
much refreshed this morning. His mind is a little weak &
flighty however. His fever is not so high. Gave him some
Laudanum this morning, which has quieted his mind a great
deal. Dozing most all day.

The 3 rd Co. moved up to join the Battalion at Bunker Hill to
day. To day they have commenced to send back the wounded &
the stores from this place.

July 20, 1863

Chaplain slept a little during last night, but is still very weak &

low. Col Walton, the Adjt & Drs. Maury & Barksdale came in & called on him. they think he will only have a day or two. Did not sleep any during the day. His mind was perfectly clear. Did not much like the idea of being left in the hands of the Yanks. Still was perfectly reconciled to anything.

To day Longstreet's Corps moved from Bunker Hill to Millwood. The whole army has commenced its backward move. Sorry we have to give up Winchester.

When I bid Chaplain "Good Night" he called me back & told me to be sure to come early in the morning.

July 21, 1863 This morning at 7 44 o'clock Mr. Chaplain died. He passed away very quietly while in a doze. He has never suffered any & has been a most patient sick man. Peace to his ashes. He was one of Natures Noblemen. & I have lost a good friend, He was buried in the cemetary at 5 1/2 P.M. amoung the Louiss His headboard said G.H. Chaplain. Wash. Artillery. Died July 21, '63.

Wrote to night to J. Bond Chaplain Cambridge Md & Mrs. A.C. Chaplain, Natchez.

Completely tired out.

A.P. Hill's Corps, passed thro' to day. Going to Front Royal.

July 22, 1863 Remained in Winchester all day. Writing letters &c. Rodes passed thro' to day. Will Holt well. Wrote T. The La Brigade will pass tomorrow so I shall remain & of on with it. as I learn it is by no means safe to go alone thro' Chester Gap. Yankee Cavalry prowling around.

July 23, 1863 Joined Genl. Harry Hays about 11 o'clk to day. Camped about 5 miles from Winchester. Not many of the Louisns left whom I know. Bill Seymour is Hays Adjt Genl. with rank of Captain. Brigade now numbers only about 900 men. Heard heavy firing toward Chester Gap this morning.

Thus I must bid farwell for an indefinite period to the luxury of sitting at a table & sleeping between clean sheets. Oh will this war never end when we can return to luxuries such as clean cloths, shirts, &c.

July 24, 1863 Started at early dawn to day toward Front Royal. Learn that the enemy got possession of the Gap yesterday evening so we had to turn back about 3 miles from Front Royal & took the road to Middletown. Camped after dark near

Strausburg. Marched about 23 miles. Enemy was skirmishing at Front Royal this mourning.

July 25, 1863 Started at Sun Rise this morning. & camped about 3 P.M. 4 miles from Mt. Jackson. Marched about 18 miles.

July 26, 1863 Left Mt. Jackson at Sun rise & camped about noon at New Market. Early's Division will cross to morrow at the Luray Gap. I met Capt. Crump at New Market & he proposed I should join him. I did so & went on to Harrisonburg. 19 miles. Met Pew. Brooks at New Market. an old school mate.

Went 30 miles to day. The Valley looks beautiful now. How soon will the hostile tread of armed men lay waste to the now peaceful homes. It makes me sad to think we have fall back from Winchester to this place.

Was sorry to leave Genl. Harry Hays & his Adjt. Capt Bill Seymour. Were very kind to me.

July 27, 1863 Broke up our Camp about 7 1/2 o'clock for Staunton. where we arrived between 12 & 1 o'clock. 25 miles. Remained here all day. Waiting for Capt. Crump to get thro' with his business. Finds he will be detained several days. So I shall send John (Chaplain's boy) with my horse to Culpepper C.H. & go on the cars.

July 28, 1863 Up bright & early. Got to the cars & found the train was an ambulance train. Succeeded in getting aboard just as they started. Saw Jusey place near Charlottesville. looks very pretty. Also saw a number of very pretty ladies at the Depot. Reached camp about 1 mile from Culpepper at 4 o'clock P.M. Glad to get back.

July 29,1863 Camp is very quiet & dull. No news of the enemy. Are said to be at Warrenton. Morgan's raid on Ohio & Indiana is the principle topic now. Dick Morgan (Col.) has been captured. He is doing immense damage to property. May success attend him & his brave followers.

July 30, 1863 John arrived in camp this morning with my horse. all safe & sound

July 31 Nothing going on of interest. Called on Miss Nettie in the evening.

Learn that Genl. John H. Morgan & all his command. with the exception of some few hundreds that escaped. were captured in Ohio. This is certainly the most daring raid of the war.

Morgan crossed into Indiana with 2500 men & 6 pieces traversed all Indiana & Ohio. Causing great alarm & making the people feel some of the terrors of war. Was finally captured by being completely surrounded by overpowering numbers.

August 1, 1863 Left camp at Culpepper C.H. at Sun rise. & halted before noon near the Rapidan River. About dark started again & camped about 5 miles across the river.

Stuart's Cavalry had a fight near Brandy to day. Our side was pushed back nearly to Culpepper C.H. when our Infantry advanced & drove the enemy back.

August 2, 1863 Encamped in the road about 2 miles from Orange C.H. in the road. Very hot. dul. very disagreeable & a very uncomfortable place.

August 3, 1863 Moved in evening to our Camp. very pleasent place.

August 10, 1863 Miller recd the offer yesterday from the Prest. thro' Col Johnson his aid of the position of Major & Chf of Arty. under Genl Preston in Western Va. Will have 22 guns there. Very pretty command.

Weather continues exceedingly hot.

August 11, 1863 Miller left for Richmond to day to see about his new appointment.[22]

August 12, 1863 Weather exceedly hot.

August 13, 1863 Rode out to Harry Hayes La Brigade to day. Have rain now every evening.

August 16, 1863 Genl. Harry Hays 1st La Brigade dined with us to day.

Miller arrived from Richmond. My Application for four days leave of absence came back to day approved.

Went out to see Miller this evening. Has his star on.

August 17, 1863 Quiet & very hot.

August 18, 1863 Started for Richmond this morning with Miller. He branched off at Gordonsville for Lynchburg & Abington. Reached Richmond at 5 1/2 P.M. Called on Miss Maggie H. in evening. Had a very pleasant visit.

Sgt. Hale left to day to ride Miller's horse "Sam" to Abingdon. distance about 270 miles.

August 19, 1863 Hard at work all day filling orders &c. Evening took a long & very agreeable walk with M.H.

August 20, 1863 Still engaged filling orders. Dined at the President's [Jefferson Davis] & took a ride on horseback after dinner with Miss M.H.

August 21, 1863 To day is the day set apart by the President for Fasting & Prayer. Went to Monumental Church with M.H. Called on Macmindo's

August 22, 1863 Finished up all my business this morning. Called on Mrs. Davis & Miss M.H. to say good bye. Also in evening on Misses Gertie & Mary.

August 23, 1863 Left Richmond to day for Camp. Arrived there at about 3 1/2 o'clk P.M.

Recieved letter to day from T. has been in camp ever since I left for R.

August 24, 1863 Ordered by Col. Walton Chf. Arty. 1st Corps. to report at his Hd Qrs. for temporary duty as Adjutant. Made vacant by Miller being promoted to Major of Artillery.

August 25, 1863 Am now duly installed as Acting Adjutant Artillery Corp. 1st Army Corps. Army of Northern Virginia.

August 26, 1863 Quiet.

Wrote T. a long & important letter.

August 27, 1863 Recd letter to day from Miller dated Abington Va 22' Inst. Genl. Preston & staff & all his Infantry had been ordered to Knoxville. Enemy reported to be advancing on that place. Left his Artillery behind but took Miller along to act as his A.A.G. in the field.

Miller reports his Arty was in bad condition, but hopes to bring order out of chaos.

August 30, 1863 A large English Whitworth Rifled Gun, weighing 22 tons, 15 inch bore, <u>600</u> pdr. has arrived at Charleston & will soon be in position to astonish the Yanks.

Went to Church to day at the Battn. Rev. Mr. Hall of N.O. preached. Has been recommended by the Major as Chaplain of the Battn.

Sept. 4, 1863 Kept rather busy in my new berth. like it, much. Wrote Maggie to day.

Sept. 8, 1863 Rec'd orders to day to move all the Artillery of Longstreet's Corps. by road to Richmond.

Genl. Longstreet's Corp is all ordered to Richmond. Thence to go reinforce Bragg in the West.

In evening the order for the Washington Artillery to move at daylight was countermanded by Genl. Longstreet.

Sept. 9, 1863 Col Walton & I left Orange C.H. this morning for Richmond by rail.

Cabell's Battalion ordered to halt at Hanover Junction until further orders.

September 12, 1863 The order for the W.A. was again revoked & they left Camp this morning at Orange C.H. for Richmond.

Sept. 13, 1863 Alexander's Batallion arrived at Richmond to day. Went in Camp on the South side of the James River. for the day. Will march to Petersburg tomorrow.

Sept. 14, 1863 Henry Battn ordered back to report to Brig. Genl. Pendelton, Chf. Arty. A.N.V. Backman's Battery (Guns, Horses & Equipment) are ordered to be turned over to Eshleman.

Sept. 15, 1863 To day at noon, the "W.A." arrived at Richmond & went on Camp at old Camp Beauregard.

Spet. 16, 1863 W. Arty. moved to the South side of the James river to camp this evening.

Sept. 17, 1863 Called at the President's home this evening with Col. Walton. Met there Miss Pollard of N.O. a beautiful young lady.

Recd letter from Miller is not very well staisfied with his present position.

Sept 18 Joe Norcom left this morning for North Carolina on furlough 7 days.

Eshleman moves to day for Petersburg.

Alexander Battn is being shipped to day from Petersburg.

Dearing's goes next & then the "W.A." All Battn & horses were ordered to leave at once, but about noon the Secy of War countermanded the order for the shipment of Dearing & Eshleman.

October 2, 1863 Left Richmond to day for Petersburg to superintend the shipment of horses from Lt. Col Branch Chf. Arty at that place. to Alexander Battn. lately sent West to Genl. Longstreet.

October 4, 1863 Shipped to day 128 horses at 3 P.M.

Petersburg a very dull place for strangers. Hotel miserable.

October 5, 1863 No shipment to day. Plenty of work & fuss.

October 6 [Shipped at 10 1/2 A.M. 152 horses & 20 mules for the West.]

The balance 40 are to be sent from Weldon.

October 7, 1863 Capt. Wood left this morning for Weldon
Shipped 132 horses & 20 mules to day at 10 1/2.
Went to W.A. Camp for a visit.
Left for Richmond this evening.

IF OWEN FOUND PETERSBURG A DULL PLACE FOR STRANGERS, he found Richmond a lively and familiar getaway, and visited there frequently in the fall and winter of 1863-1864. Between October 7th and 14th (his last entry before December 1st), Owen called on "Mrs. Davis & the young ladies" and enjoyed other social opportunities and excursions.

December 1 Starvation club Party to-night at Miss Constance
Cary's failure.
Went to-day on the Flag of Truce Str. "Shultz". with a large party — Col. Ould & lady. Mrs. Genl. Randolph, Miss Maggie Howell, Misses Lee, Mrs. Semmes, Ives, Meyers, Misses Preston &c. Capt. Bayot of the French vessel of war "Grenade" was aboard. Reached the "Grenade" at City Point about 2 P.M. dranks lots of champagne & then returned.

December 3, 1863 Took a ride on horse back with Miss Truxie J.[23] to Chaffin's Bluff. Just after we left her house on Clay & 3rd St. her horse took fright & started to run away. & went down 3rd St. towards Gamble Hill. I succeeded in stopping him just as he reached the edge of the prescipice.

December 7, 1863 Col Walton recieved orders to day to go to Petersburg & there make his Hd Qrs. & take immediate command of the W.A. & Dearings Battn

December 8, 1863 Starvation Club Party to night at Miss Herndon's I went with Trux
Enjoyed myself much.

December 10, 1863 Col. Walton & I left Richmond to day to make Hd Qrs. in Petersburg. near the two Battalions of Longstreets Corps. Do not like the change at all.

OWEN GOT TO RICHMOND TWICE IN THE ENSUING WEEK, accompanying Trux to church and to a party. "Enjoyed myself."

December 17, 1863 Capt. Miller ordered off to-day to Lynchburg, to report to Genl. Nickols. Yankee Cavalry under Averill having tapped the R.R. to Bristol at Salem about 60 miles from Lynchburg.

Major Dearing left to day with over 100 men of his Battn. equipped as Cavalry. to pursue a raiding party of Yanks about the Blackwater.

Called early in R. on J. ns. Had a very pleasant time indeed.

December 18, 1863 Left Richmond early this morning for Petersburg.

Miller came with me, having recd orders to report to S.W. Va District to take command of all the Guns in the District.

December 21, 1863 Washn. Arty moved to day to the Model Farm near Petersburg.

December 24, 1863 Remained in Richmond to partake of some Egg Nog at Mrs. Davis'.

December 31, 1863 Went to Richmond to night to spend New Years day.

January 1, 1864 Called at the President's[.] Mrs. Semmes, Mrs. Enders, Miss Pegram, Miss Palmers, Miss Giles, Miss Cary. Evening—Went to party at Mrs. Johnson's.

January 2, 1864 Intended returning to Petersburg today, but Mrs. Davis and Mrs. Semmes insisted on my remaining to take part in some tableaux and pantomimes at Mrs. S's on Thursday night.

Januaruy 7, 1864 Pantomimes took place to night at Mrs. Semmes. I took 4 characters Were a decided success. the plays I mean

January 8, 1864 Returned to Petersburg this afternoon. brought Truxie Johnson & Miss Enders. Heavy snow storms to day.

January 17, 1864 Took a walk with Miss Truxie. back of town. had a long chat sitting under a tree in a valley

༄

VII. Letters of Sgt. George Apps and Cpl. Fred Brode to Josephine Trinchard, 1863-1865

Fred Brode to Josephine Trinchard, undated fragment, ca. Christmas 1863

I wish you could see me now. I am a pretty hard looking case, a regular <u>hard-up</u> confederate. But when I go out, I have anything at my service, that my mess have got, in the shape of dry goods. I borrow one's Boots, another one's hat, another ones shirt and neck-tie and white collar and so you see I get along quite well as long as we are stationed here. I go to church every Sunday, weather permitting. Don't ~~drin~~ drink any liquors, stronger than water as if confederate shinplasters are too scarce (not because the liquor is too scarce) did not ever have a drop to drink on Christmas or New Years. Did not taste Egg-nogg. But I don't mind that, I can get along very well with good Spring water, and we have any quantity of that here. We have not had any snow here yet, but it has been so cold that the Ponds have been frozen thick enough to have skating. (ice 3 inches thick)

. . . Tell Ma and Pa that I thought of them on their birthdays, what a pleasant time we used to have, And we, our mess often talk how, first one would say I would like to have a cup of Chockalate, and another a nice cup of good coffee and ~~Soon~~ soon. But you know we are in this little thing called war and we must stick it out to the very last man Well it is getting late, and I am going to bed and try to dream of home any how. Joe do send me all you can by Mr. Haile[24] please, if only the hat and watch and the pipe. I wish you would get me a nice little merchaum pipe for my Christmas gift God bless and protect you all, and I hope ~~yet~~ we may yet see each other soon. . . .

Your Brother
F.A.B.

∾

Winter Quarters, Petersburg, Jany 6. '64
Dr Sister Joe:
I think I have one more chance of sending you a letter Should the Young man by whom I send this, deliver it himself, I wish you would ask him in, and he will tell you all about me, and Ned Apps and James Edwards, and William Martin, and You can see their

folks, and let them know how they are getting along. I told him to see you before he came back and if profible, You can give him for me any little thing that You may wish to send me. . . . In my last three or four letters, I have asked for several small things that I wish you would send me thinking that at least one of them would reach you. If this young man Mr Slvt [Sylvester] Haile to the house I wish you would ask him to bring me out a good felt hat. I have not had a hat since last winter, except what some of my mess mates gave me. He told me he could not bring me out any large package, but if you will ask him, I think he would do it for you. I wish you would also send me out my watch, after having [got?] it in good runing order. If you can send me also a good pipe and about a dozen U.S. postage stamps, so that I can write to you by flag of truce. I hope that you will not think that I am asking for to much, but if you only knew how hard it is to get any thing in the Confederacy, you would not think hard of it, I am sure. I did, in my other letters ask for shoes, toilet, soap, a couple pf good combs, and a couple of hats, but unless you had a great deal of good luck I do not know how you could send them, ~~unless it was to~~]. A Young man; Mr S. Turner rec'd a box from New Orleans, by way of Mobile, last week I also asked for some under and over-shirts, and socks. Just think; we get only $12. per month, and a pair of shoes cost $100. a hat $80.oo to $100.oo. I bought two cakes of soap, such as they make here the other day, and had to pay $2.oo a piece. Confederate Money of the old issue will be called in, and will not be worth any thing after the first day of April So if there is any at home, I wish You would send me out some. . . .

We are very comfortablly fixed here for the winter, and will re-main here until ~~next~~ next May I think. Our Christmas and New Years passed off here just the same as any other day. Only that one of my mess mates got a fine large turkey and 3 wild ducks for Chrismas dinner. On New Years' day I went out in the country and dined out with some acquaintances that I made. Every time I go there I am welcomes. There are three old maids there the Youngest about 25 and the oldest about 30. and they have invited; to come out there and go to Church with them and when we get home to dine and spend the day there. I have a very nice time when I go there and it aways makes me think of home. . . .

M. Page Lapham
The Museum of the Confederacy

Camp Washington Artillery
Petersburg, Va. Mch 24th 1864
Dear Sister:

Having still another chance to send you another letter I take the opportunity of sending you one. Since I rec'd your letter by Mr. Haile, I have sent you two, this makes the third; I have no news to send you. The snow that fell day before Yesterday makes the roads so disagreeable that I hate to go to town now. If you wish to write me often, I wish you would write by flag of truce and I can receive a letter every 10 or 20 days. . . . After having addressed my letter in one envelope, with a confederate postage Stamp, put it into another envelope, and addressed thus. "To Commandant of U.S. Forces, Virginia and North Carolina, Fort Monroe." and at the top put "<u>By Flag of truce</u>". With "Yankee Postage stamp". and when you send such a letter don't write more than one page of letter on foolscap paper, ~~and~~ speak about write nothing, about confederate or Yankee armies. Also, send two or three Yankee postage stamps so that I can answer your letter. Tell Pa that Lieut Brown[25] has returned, & looks very well. Also Mr. Wm. Hall and brother & Jas. Edwards and Ned Apps. I wish you would get me some money if Ma can give it without interfering with her. As I have borrowed about a hundred and fifty Dolls. and cant pay unless I get some from home. I had to get this to supply some of my wants in the way of clothing. But I don't think that I am suffering, for I am too smart for that, I think. I suppose when you have seen my likeness you will think so. I told Rodolph to ask Mr. Jones to send me out a hundred or two Dollars in gold or greenbacks, I do not know whether he will do it or not. If Mr. Early comes to you for anything Mr. Price is the name of the gentleman by whom I send this.. . .

Your affectionate
Brother, Fred.

VIII. The Death of M. Page Lapham

Cut off as it was from its home city, the Washington Artillery after April 1862 recruited new members from other states. Joining the unit in August 1863 was a 17-year-old student from Danville, Virginia, M. Page Lapham. He served as a private in Capt. J. B. Richardson's 2nd company.[26] Two documents relating to his service survive among Richardson's papers donated to The Museum of the Confederacy. On April 1, 1864, Richardson granted Lapham "permission to visit Danville to return in five (5) days." The other document is a letter written by Richardson to Lapham's mother a few months later:

> Camp Near Petersburg. Virginia
> September 7th 1864   Battery No. 35
>
> Mrs. Lapham.
> Danville Va.
> Dear Madam
> I send to day to Capt. McKenzie Louisiana Depot Richmond a small box The property of your gallant son M. Page Lapham, once an honorable member of my Company who was Killed while gallantly discharging His Duty at the battle of Drury's Bluff May 14th 1864 [sic. May 16th]. This is the only things of his that I have been able to find and have taken care of it Knowing that you would be pleased to have it sent to you.
> Allow me to say that his deportment during his connection with my Company was everything that could be desired obedient, respectful and gentlemanly, with all the highest Sense of honor and brave chivalrance and daring on the battlefield.
> It is not my good fortune to have the pleasure of a personal acquaintance with you but from the warm and intimate association of your Son and myself I take the liberty of addrressing you this note and in conclusion allow me as his commanding officer to extend to you my heart's fullest sympathy for your loss of this gallant Boy.
> The Country has been deprived of one of its noblest and bravest defenders and his memory Shall ever be dear to myself and every member of my Company.
> Very Respectfully

J.B. Richardson
Capt comdg 2nd Company
Washington Artillery

IX. The Letters of Edward Apps and Fred Brode (continued)

Fred Brode to Josephine Brode Trinchard
Petersburg July 26, 1864
Dear Sister

... I will be one among the first to get a furlough, next winter, and if I have a chance, I will try and go to New Orleans. I will go as far as Mobile and when I get there I can see whether I can go further or not. I have several invitations to spend a month or more, at the homes of some of my friends, but I declined, for fear I might not be able to go home, should I have an opportunity.

Old Grant is still in front of us and I suppose intends to spend the remainder of the summer, and perhaps a part of next fall with us. But his company is anything but agreeable to us. He is always throwing large 30 pounder shells into town, which is very uncomfortable. All the people have moved from the lower end of town to the upper part and are living in tents or sheds. A great many are living in tents, and are fixed very comfortable. It is very hard to remove Grant from where he is, as he has the Appomattox on his right flank, and the James in his rear. But he cannot advance any nearer to town, as there is a little wall in his way, that is Lee's line. Both sides are throwing mortar shells at each other. They look like sky rockets, where they go off through the air.

We had a very nice little fight here in front of our lines where our Battalion is, about four weeks ago in which we took 1742 prisoners, besides killed and wounded. We captured 4 pieces of Artillery. We took them by surprise having flanked them on their left. You may imagine what a surprise it must have been, when they actually left their muskets stacked in the trenches. I came very near "going up the spout," myself at this fight. After the Fight, I went out in to see how things looked, and to see also, how many killed and wounded there were. I had gone as far as our line of battle was, when all of a sudden the Yanks made a charge to retake their works, (in which they failed however) when they fired a volley the minie' balls flying all around me. I thought this was no place for me so I got up and ran as fast as I could. While running to the rear I had to cross the artillery fire of the Yankees, and their shells burst all around me. I did not mind that much, but one of their shells passed within one yard in front of my body, bursting just as it had passed me. It was a very narrow escape, and proves to me that one never dies until his time comes. This is the third time that I had such a narrow escape. We have not had any other fight here since the above. We have a great deal of Artillery firing, and some picket firing on our left, especially at night. In front of us, there is no firing. The pickets exchange papers, and our boys also give them tobacco for sugar, coffee soap &c..&c. But even this has been stopped and I am very glad of it, as it gives the men too much chance to desert. Any men seen going in front of the line of pickets is to be shot.

I have quite an easy time just now. My Sargeant was wounded at Drewry's Bluff fight and we lost so many horses that we only have three guns now. If we were to get enough horses for another gun, I would act as a sargeant. We have had a very dry spell here. Very hot and dusty until yesterday When we had a slight shower. I hope that this fall they decide the fate of this war, and give us peace once more. I should not be surprised if the next Presidential Campaign will settle this thing I do not believe that the people in the North will stand it much North [sic.]. They are getting tired of the war I think.

F.A.B.

∽

Petersburg, Va. November 2, 1864
4th Co Battalion Washington Artillery

Dear Sister Joe
Yours of the 2d October came to hand on the evening of the 2d of Nov. just 31 days coming. If I could only get a letter from home once a monthing how well pleased I would be, but when I

get one it seems to me to be an age until I get another. You say that you have written me about six letters via Fortress Monroe if so I have not received a single one, and you had better not write by that way any more, for I believe the Yankee rascals open the letters and steal the stamps and burn or destroy the letters This is the first letter that I rec'd from you for six months. . . .

I rec'd Pauline's Photograph. The face seems as familiar to me as if it had been but yesterday that I saw her at home. As familiar as when we were all at home together when all was peace and happiness. When I think of those happy days but nevermind. I hope everything will be all right yet, and that shortly too There is one consolation, and that is the war can't last forever. Time has passed by very fast. It hardly seems to me that I have been out here four years, but it certainly is so. When we left home we thought it would be a pleasure trip for three months. We have been here more than so many years. I would be very well satisfied, if old Jeff and Lincoln would settle up, and let us all go home and leave a civilized life once more. But so long as this lasts, and so long as I am able, I am willing to do all I can. I would not want to have a discharge from the Army to go home and remain, if it was offered to me. But I would like to spend a couple of weeks there. In my last letters, I was telling you that you need not be surprised if you saw me come a peeping in some day, but I would be very much surprised, now, if such were the case. I have changed my mind. The commandant at New Orleans is a little too strict now, and besides our officers have become more strict also. Every one reeceiving a Furlough now, has to take an oath that he will not enter the enemy's lines. But I think if I have luck, that I shall go as far as Moblie, and visit some of my friends there Lucius P. has given me an invitation some time ago.

We are very comfortably fixed here for the coming winter. All of our boys are building log cabins for themselves. Ours has been finished already for a week. We do our own Cooking now. I am cook in the morning and one of my mess mates cooks dinner. The other three of my mess divide the balance of the work. Ned Apps sleeps in our house. We have a very nice little fire place and in the evening we all get around and have a nice little chat until bed time, which is quite early, 7 1/2 o'clock. I got all the boys to go to bed earlier to-night so that I could write these letters, for the

room is so small when we are all up that no body can do anything.
. . .

I am very sorry to hear that Theodore is in prison. If he has to leave home, I would like for him to come direct here. If he should go via Mobile they will try to conscript him there, but he can let them know where he came from. Any one under the age of conscription, and coming from the enemies lines, has the privilege of joining anything that he chooses. Besides he can enquire for Lucius there and he will tell him what to do. If he has to come he can enlist in Mobile for Capt Joe Norcom's Co.4th Co B.W.A. And if he wants to see Lucius, let him enquire for the 22d La. Reg't.[27]

I will send his letter by way of Clinton La. . . .

Brother

"Fred."

P.S. Some of the Black from off the candle fell on this page, and dirtied it somewhat after I had the letter written, but you must overlook it, as paper is both very dear and very scarce.

[written on the last page up the left hand side from the first Post Script]

Heavy Artillery, Mortar & Musketry firing going on just now. It is 12 o'clock at night, All of our boys had to get up, but it will not Amount to anything I believe, We often have this false alarms.

∽

Fort Louisiana
4th Co. Battalion W.A.
Petersburg, Nov. 19th 1864

Dear Sister Joe

Having another opportunity I will again write you a few lines, by a friend who is going home to Clinton, La.

I wrote you a long letter on the 5th Nov. which I hope you will have received, in which I gave you a description of our house and our comfortable situatation for the coming winter, providing that we are allowed to remain here.

We have had some very pleasant weather here for the last two months, but today is a very disagreable day- rainey, cold and muddy. I am pretty well fixed for cold weather as far as clothes is concerned. I have a good Yankee over coat given to me by one of my mess, also a good vest two new shirts, made for me by the ladies that I have mentioned to You Misses Hawkes. They are making me some good woolen socks. They have not charged me for any thing so far. The socks, are very nice. Those ladies have been very kind to me, and have done a great deal for me. You must not think that it is because, I am love with any of them, that they are doing for me what they have done for they are old Maids, except one, and she is engaged. What they have done for me is only through friendship; they seem to have taken a great fancy to me. I was at their house Yesterday and had three glasses of splendid butter milk. Before they were driven from their homes in the Country, I used to get as much as I wanted. But they live in town now, and feel the effects of the war as much as anybody. . . .

F.A.B.

∼

Fort Louisiana" Near Petersburg
December 26th 1864

Hoping you have had a merry Christmas and happy New Years. I address you these few lines hoping they will find you enjoying good health. I wrote to you on the 14th of October by Flag of truce, in answer to your letter of the 19th of September. Since Sherman has been passing through Georgia, the communication with the South has been very uncertain. I have not had a letter from Bertrand or Charles for over a month, they were both well when I last heard from them.

Yesterday I spent in camp; it was the dullest, and bluest Christmas that I have ever seen since the beginning of the war, But I hope next year that I will be able to eat my Christmas dinner in New Orleans, and though I may have a poor dinner, Still the pleasure of eating it with friends and relatives will make up for the dinner. Fred has not had a letter from you, for seven months, the last he received was by Mr. Price. The yanks fired a salute of one hundred guns this morning opposite to our fort,) in honor of the evacuation of Savannah by our troops, and the possession of it by Sherman. . . .

Fort Louisiana
Petersburg Va, Dec 27th 1864.
Dear Sister Joe
I hope you have all had a merry Christmas and will have a Happy New Year. As for myself and mess I must say considering the times, we had an excellent Christmas Dinner, and I had the pleasure of cooking it. We had Roast Pork boiled and sweet potatoes, and apple dumplings till you could'nt see. It is the first time that I ever amused myself making any Dumplings and we had sauce made of melted butter, and sugar with a little nutmeg. What we will have for a New Years Dinner, God only Knows, but I hope it will be something beside rations, as they would be rather slim.
Fred
Fort Louisiana

∽

4th Co Battalion Washington Artillery
Petersburg Va, Jany 7th 1865

Dear Sister Joe
. . . We had a pretty good time here on Christmas Day, but a poor New Years'. Besides having a poor Dinner (corn bread and Bacon) it was a nasty rainy, raw cold day.

The Yankees keep quiet here now. There has been no shelling for some time, nothing but picket firing, and that only at night.

We have had tolerable good weather so far. Only two - Snow storms, and not very much Cold weather. I hope it may continue so, as I am not very fond of the cold weather, and it is very severe on the poor infantry that have to stand picket guard.

Mr. Frederick Ames[28] has gone from here on furlough, and I think may go to N. Orleans if he should; I wish you would get him to fetch me a hat. (Soft felt hat, about Pa's fit) and get him to take it as I am very much in need of one

Brother
Frederick.

～

George Edward Apps to Josephine Brode Trinchard

Fort Louisiana Near Petersburg Va
January 19, 1865

Your long and very interesting letter dated December 6th has been received, and its contents read with a great deal of pleasure. I commenced to think that I had been forgotten by all my friends; it has been so long since I heard from any of them.

In your letter "you say I must be getting tired of my pleasure trip which has lasted so long." I am certainly getting tired of staying away from home and all my friends, but I come out for a purpose and untill that object is accomplished, (our independence gained) I shall have to deprive myself of the pleasure of seeing my friends in visiting my home. But I hope with all my heart that the day is not far distant, when the Southern Confederacy will be a free and independent nation, and this cruel war will have ended. Then what joy there will be when friends and relatives will meet not to be parted again untill God doth call us to our final home. Then indeed will it give me pleasure to relate anicdotes, and give accounts of battles that I have been fortunate enough to go through, and if it is in my power I shall be glad to hear your hearty laugh, and if I can releive the minds of any of my friends, and make them forget the past. I will indeed enjoy a hearty laugh.

We cant give any more dramatic performances this season, nearly all the performers have been killed or wounded in the last campaign. What few are left dont feel in the humor. In answer to your questions "Are there any pretty ladies here"? Yes. plenty. "Have you found your better half yet"? No. I have not taken the trouble of looking around, as I hope to find some New Orleans girl that remains true to the cause, And I dont think it right I that we should all forget our fair friends at home. I think I shall commission you to hunt me up a sweet heart so that I shant have any trouble hunting one up when the war is over. Of course you will have to give me a good recommendation, or as the "Irish say, a good "Car-acter."

I hope Josephine has recovered from her late sickness. I see by your letter Jos. _____ has three boys, I hope Joe will bring them up in the right cause, and if this war should last long enough; they may have to put their shoulders to the wheel, and keep the wagon going.

News was unusually scarce yesterday. Not a word of any thing doing. The yankees fired a salute of one hundred guns yesterday, to let us know they had captured "Fort Fisher" Near Wilmington but I think it was a wast of powder. But I suppose they have to resort to such dodges to keep up the spirits of their Army.

Since the fall of Savannah, and Sherman march through Georgia, and Hood defeat at Nashville, and now the fall of Fort Fisher, our cause does not look as bright as I had hoped it would at the close of the campaign. But thanks to God, the yankees have gained nothing from this army, its reputation is still untarnished, and Grant with his motly crew, dread the idea of what a reception they will get, when they come forth to battle with us. They have been handled so roughly by the army of Northern Virginia, that it is with the greatest difficulty that their officers can get them to charge our men. Our lines in front of Petersburg are in some places only fifty or sixty yards apart, but still the yankees dare not try to drive us out. I expect when the spring campaign opens we will have a very hot time here. Both yanks and Confeds have mortar batteries along the lines, and amuse themselves by exchanging shots, just imagin shells 8 and 10 inches in diameter dropping as it were from the skies, coming down amongst a lot of men; You can imagin what a scatteration they make, sometimes burying themselves four feet in the Earth and then bursting, it looks like a small Volcano.

Ed,

Fort Louisiana
Petersburg Va Jan'y 29th '65

Dear Sister
. . . Everything is very quiet along the lines in front and around Petersburg. I suppose Grant intends to wait until spring before he will make any more moves.

I am and have been working at my old Business (printing) since the 13th of Sept. I got permission from my Capt and Col. I told them it was for the purpose of buying myself some clothes. But everything is so high here, that it would take a cart load of confederate money to buy a suit of clothes. I get Ten Dollars per day and am boarded, that is I get my breakfast and Dinner, and whenever I remain in town over night I stop at Mr Campbell's house (one of the propretors of the Daily Petersburg Express) and get a good bed and supper. Counting every thing I get about - or what is equal to One hundred and Sixty Dollars per week - as board is one hundred per week. I have not all that I want to get. A hat - that is a good one - cannot be had in this town or Confederacy, I believe. The kind they have, the ask three hundred for and Shoes $250. I got a pair of shoes - but they are too light. Socks are Ten Dolls per pair. Jos. You see everything is very high.

We are very comfortable in out house, having enough of wood to last us for the winter. I believe. Besides, we yet 5 bushels of coal to a man, and as here are six in our mess, we rec'd 30 bushels, which, with the wood, will last us a month, when we will get more. We have a grate, so arranged that we can take it out and burn wood in the mornings - so as to cook our breakfast and Dinner, and those being the only meals we have - not having enough rations for a supper - we put in our grate and enjoy a nice coal fire after dinner until bed time. . . .

Your Brother
Fred.

The Washington Artillery spent the miserable winter of 1864-1865 in the trenches around Petersburg. When the Confederate disaster at Five Forks on April 1, 1865 compelled Lee to abandon Petersburg, the

Washington Artillery was charged with holding the key position at Fort Gregg. In one of its bloodiest and fiercest engagements of the war, the unit held the fort most of April 2. The Washington Artillery then fell back from Petersburg and moved toward Appomattox Court House.

Fred Brode, Ned Apps, Edward and William Miller Owen and John B. Richardson survived the war and apparently remained with the Washington Artillery in its postwar incarnations. Richardson rose to the rank of colonel and was the battalion commander between 1880 and 1896. He had the distinction of being the owner of Everett B. D. Julio's famous painting, "The Last Meeting of Lee and Jackson," which he displayed in the Washington Artillery arsenal. Richardson died in 1906 and was mourned as an "earnest, chivalrous and independent" man, who "was what he seemed to be."[29]

After the war, Edward Owen joined Gen. James Longstreet in a business partnership. Owen's cotton business took him to New York City, where he became a member of the Cotton Exchange and an active member in that city's business community and Democratic Party leadership. Not forgetting his regional loyalties, Owen helped to found a New York camp of the United Confederate Veterans and was the camp's long-time leader. Forsaking Maggie and Trux and his other wartime flirtations, Owen married in 1866 to Hattie Bryan. Following her death, he married again in 1874. At the time of his death in 1919, Owen was survived by one daughter.[30]

Notes

1. Originally published in 1875; reprinted by Louisiana State University Press in 1964 for the Civil War Centennial. See also Powell A. Casey, *An Outline of the Civil War Campaigns and Engagements of the Washington Artillery of New Orleans* (Baton Rouge, 1986).

2. James M. McPherson, *Why They Fought* (Baton Rouge, 1994).

3. Owen, *In Camp and Battle*, p. 11.

4. Biographies of Richardson in *Washington Artillery Souvenir* (New Orleans, ca. 1894), p. 8; obituary from *New Orleans Picayune* reprinted in *Confederate Veteran*, vol. 14(1906), p. 130.

5. *Records of Louisiana Confederate Soldiers and Louisiana Confederate Commands,* compiled by Andrew B. Booth (New Orleans, 1920), vol. I, pp. 71, vol. II, p. 125. Hereinafter cited as *Records,* volume: (part), page; "Roll of Honor," vol. 85, p. 12, Eleanor S. Brockenbrough Library, The Museum of the Confederacy.

6. Biographical information on Josephine Brodé Trinchard from *New Orleans Picayune,* reprinted in *Richmond Times-Dispatch,* November 24, 1912, in CMLS Scrapbook, 1912-1915, p. 21, Eleanor S. Brockenbrough Library, The Museum of the Confederacy. "Sketch of Service of Corporal F.B. Trinchard," in Kate Mason Rowland Papers, Eleanor S. Brockenbrough Library, The Museum of the Confederacy.

7. Camp "Orleans," into which the battalion moved on September 1, 1861, turned out to be headquarters for only six weeks. W. M. Owen, *In Camp and Battle,* p. 53, 58; Richardson's diary also detailed changes in camp and locations of each company.

8. The 7th Louisiana Infantry, commanded by Col. Harry Hays, was part of the Louisiana Brigade in the Army of Northern Virginia. Seven of the regiment's ten companies, including the Crescent City Rifles (companies E and H) and the Continental Guards (company A), were raised in New Orleans. Arthur W. Bergeron, Jr., *Guide to Louisiana Military Units 1861-1865* (Baton Rouge, 1989), 87-88.

9. Joseph Trinchard was listed on the rolls of Company C, Orleans Cadets in

June 1861, several months before it became Company I, 18th Louisiana Infantry. Records, III, 2, p. 871; Bergeron, *Guide,* pp.119-120.

10. Walton's promotion to chief of artillery of the Army of the Potomac (as the future Army of Northern Virginia was then called) did not take him away from the Washington Artillery. In 1862, he assumed command of the artillery of Maj.Gen. James Longstreet's wing (later corps) of the Army of Northern Virginia. Only in March 1863 did Walton yield command of the battalion to Maj. Benjamin Franklin Eshleman, the commander of 1st Company who was wounded in the unit's first action at Blackburn's Ford on July 18, 1861, then returned to service as commander of the 4th Company.

11. Martin, a 26-year-old New Orleans carpenter, enlisted originally in the 16th Mississippi Infantry, and was transferred to 4th Company, Washington Artillery on December 27, 1861. He was wounded at the battle of Drewry's Bluff on May 16, 1864, and returned to Louisiana, where he took the oath of allegiance to the Federal government. *Records,* vol. III, p. 900.

12. Owen, *In Camp,* pp. 189-190, 194.

13. Records, vol. III, part 2, p. 52; *Confederate Veteran,* vol. 27(March 1919), p. 107; *Souvenir,* p. 7. Sources do not agree on the brothers' birth dates or on who was the eldest. Edward, apparently the younger, was in his mid-twenties at the beginning of the war, William in his late twenties.

14. Jefferson Davis, letter of June 8, 1870.

15. *Blue & Gray,* vol. II(1893), pp. 43-44.

16. Margaret and Jenny Howell were sisters of Confederate first lady Varina Howell Davis. Maggie (1842-1930) was one of Richmond's most eligible belles, and, because of her plain-spoken manner, one of the most trying for her suitors. In 1870, she married Chevalier Charles de Wechmar Stoess, a German consul in England. And while she spent her life traveling, she never lost touch with the Owen brothers, who reportedly gave her a piece of the Washington Artillery's battle flag. Christine de Wechmar Stoess, "Episodes in the Life of Margaret Graham Howell, Madame de Wechmar Stoess," compiled by Lorraine Chapman, unpublished manuscript, ca. 1934, in White House of the Confederacy research files, Richmond, VA.

17. Capt. Joseph Norcom, a 28-year old North Carolina born clerk, enlisted as a lieutenant and rose to command of the 4th Company in 1862. He was wounded at Gettysburg, July 3, 1863. *Records,* III:1, p. 1294.

18. William Miller Owen (*In Camp and Battle,* p. 204) noted that his brother was in the neighborhood and even acknowledged his prowess with the ladies: "My brother. . . is sojourning at Montgomery, and came down to see me, and I have promised to return with him. He offers special inducements, promising to introduce me to some lovely girls.

19. Private Morgan E. Harris, veteran of an undetermined regiment, enlisted in 1st Company, Washington Artillery, on April 1, 1863. Since Harris was also an Ohio native, Morgan's acquaintance with Owen may have been a long one; it ended, however, in July 1864 when Harris was killed at Petersburg. *Records,* III:1, p. 203.

20. Myra Eulalie Knox Semmes and her husband, Louisiana senator Thomas J. Semmes, lived during the war in the Bruce-Lancaster house, across Clay and

12th streets from the Confederate executive mansion. "A born actress," Mrs. Semmes made her rented quarters one of the social centers of wartime Richmond. See Thomas Cooper DeLeon, "Belles, Beaux and Brains of the `60s" (New York, 1908), Chapter IX; "Honorable Thomas J. Semmes," *Southern Historical Society Papers,* vol. 25(1897), p. 326.

21. Edward Owen's account of the battle of Chancellorsville is published in William Miller Owen's *In Camp and Battle,* pp. 228-229.

22. On August 10, 1863, William Miller Owen was offered a promotion to major as chief of artillery of the district of South-West Virginia. He remained in Southwest Virginia and Tennessee until April 1864, when he returned to the Washington Artillery as second in command of the battalion. Owen, *In Camp,* pp. 263ff; *Souvenir,* p. 7.

23. Owen's most frequent female companion was Mary Truxton Johnston—"`Truxie' to half of the State," recalled Navy Department clerk Thomas Cooper DeLeon. Despite, perhaps because of her reputation as a well-traveled wartime belle, "Truxie" Johnston never married. DeLeon, "Belles," Chapter X.

24. A frequent courier of mail for Fred Brode, Sylvester T. Haile enlisted as a private in the 4th Company and was promoted in April 1863 to quartermaster sergeant. He was listed as absent sick in the hospital at Petersburg between November 1863 and February 1864, but evidently visited Louisiana during that absence. He was absent sick again from Aug 28, 1864 through February 1865. *Records,* vol. III, p. 152.

25. Lt. Charles H.C. Brown of 1st Company was captured at Gettysburg, imprisoned at Johnson's Island Ohio, and Pt. Lookout, Maryland, then paroled and exchanged at City Point, Virginia, on March 16, 1864. *Records,* vol. II, p. 142.

26. *Records,* Vol. III:I, p. 658.

27. Lt. A. Lucius Plattsmier, Jr., of New Orleans, was a member of the 22nd (Consolidated) Louisiana Infantry. *Records,* III, 2, p. 159.

28. Cpl. Fred W. Ames, 4th Company, was listed as absent on furlough from December 28, 1864. *Records,* vol. I, p. 56.

29. Obituary in *Confederate Veteran.*

30. Ibid.

Book Reviews

The Confederate Republic: A Revolution Against Politics, by George C. Rable (University of North Carolina Press, P.O. Box 2288, Chapel Hill, NC 27515-2288) 1994. B&W photographs, notes, bibliography, index. 416pp. Cloth. $34.95

Of thousands of volumes written about the Civil War, only a few focus on the political and philosophical arenas of the conflict. Traditional biographies offer glimpses into these realms, but in-depth discussions are rare. In Southern historiography, political philosophy and its application typically are pictured only as hastening the end of the war.

George C. Rable's *The Confederate Republic,* subtitled *A Revolution Against Politics, is* a long overdue work that any serious student of Southern history and the Civil War should welcome. Rable attempts to define Confederate political culture as a separate entity, and he succeeds admirably. Utilizing hundreds of manuscripts, Confederate and individual state documents, newspapers, periodicals, sermons, and secondary sources, the author portrays Southern political life in a totally fresh approach.

Southern politicians considered themselves the true heirs of the American Revolution. They felt that the United States and its political structure had been contaminated beyond repair by party politics and a pervasive view in Washington toward federalism. The evolution of issue-oriented political parties in the United States and their need to identify with voters (particularly the abolitionists) infuriated the South.

As the movement toward secession gathered momentum, Southerners began to define what had gone wrong with the country and what remedies were best. Southern society attempted to define itself as a new, pure form of culture. The new Confederate system was viewed from within, as the subtitle suggests, as a revolution against politics. This revolution was rabidly anti-party and pious. At its core was the view that unity among whites negated the need for the trappings of government as practiced in Washington.

The author's chronological method of examining his subject allows the reader to see how the Confederate government, the states, individual politicians, ministers, and newspapers affected policy and were, in turn, changed by the war. The themes that recur throughout the work are the positions taken by nationalists and the libertarians and the pro- and anti-Jefferson Davis factions. Civil libertarians were always suspicious of any attempt to create a strong central government, and the nationalists were constantly frustrated over individual states trying to exercise their authority over policy and their own troops. The need for military considerations as the war progressed exacerbated these problems. Appointments of political generals hurt both sides in the war, but the South was at times paralyzed by them, particularly in the West.

Positions taken by the nationalists and the libertarians naturally influenced opinions among the citizenry regarding the conduct of the president and the Confederate Congress. The influence of large circulation newspapers and sermons from the pulpits of prominent ministers added greatly to the debate. Rable contends that the internal bickering should "not be used to explain the outcome of the war but rather should serve as a window through which to examine the political nature of the Southern revolution" (p. 300).

As the war progressed and the tide turned against the Confederates, political debates turned to loss of individual liberty (particularly the suspension of *habeas corpus),* the arming and use of blacks as soldiers, and the emancipation of those slaves in return for military service. These issues—typically relegated to an aside in most studies—provide a fresh and interesting view of Southern politics.

Rable approaches his subject by describing the positions taken by prominent Southerners, detailing the manner in which they influenced events and showing how these positions changed as outside factors affected circumstances. Events in the war are treated as the primary altering influence, and to illustrate these changes the reader is treated to concurrent mini-biographies of various Southern luminaries, including Jefferson Davis and Attorney General Judah P. Benjamin. Also presented are excellent portraits of Joseph E. Brown, Howell Cobb, Thomas Cobb, John M. Daniel, William Graham, Benjamin Hill, William Holden, Robert Rhett, Edmund Ruffin, Alexander Stephens, Robert Toombs, Zebulon Vance, Thomas Watts, Louis T. Wigfall, and William

Lowndes Yancey, and others.

If the Southerners' passion for their concept of individual liberty, distrust of party politics, and a deeply ingrained anathema for centralized federal government ended with the capture and imprisonment of Jefferson Davis, the study of Confederate political culture would be all but useless. The author contends that these values remained long after war and that the emerging white ruling class carried these tenets long after the war. Post Civil War political history in the South, extending even to the present, affirms Rable's position.

Rable's writing style is systematic and intellectual. The academic styling and verbiage of introductory chapters may discourage readers who are not highly motivated to learn more about this subject. However, even an unmotivated reader will find something of interest once he passes through the preliminary material. By the third chapter the book begins to read almost like a novel of people and events. Rable should be commended for his clear direction and his ability to view objectively those about whom he writes. The book is free of bias as the author avoids over-glorification or condemnation of the personalities of the times.

The Confederate Republic: A Revolution Against Politics is insightful, thoroughly researched, and well written. The volume is valuable not only for its contribution to Civil War literature in general, but for covering a much neglected facet of the period. Rable's text is fully documented, and his prose flows smoothly. His extensive list of sources, particularly the unpublished manuscripts and various Confederate government and individual state sources will be helpful to researchers. This volume will be a welcome addition to any Civil War library.

GARY JOINER
SHREVEPORT, LA

Landscapes of the Civil War, Constance Sullivan (Alfred A. Knopf, Inc., 201 E. 50th St., New York, NY 10022) 1995, B&W photos, plates, preface. 145pp. Cloth. $40.00.

There is an intriguing story behind this book. The Medford Historical Society in Massachusetts moved into its present building in 1916, where it has maintained a museum ever since. In 1990, a schoolchild who had taken a class tour returned home and told his father about the interesting Civil War items on display. The father, a Civil War buff, subsequently visited the museum, enjoyed seeing the artifacts, and talked with the Society's curator about their mutual interests in history. The curator mentioned an old wooden chest kept in the storage area of the building which contained a number of uncatalogued, unrestored albumen prints, apparently made from Civil War-era photographic plates. Although the museum's staff had known about them, no effort had been made to organize the historic prints or publicize them to historians. After examining the photographs, approximately fifty-four hundred in number, the two men decided to consult a specialist to ascertain the historical importance of the collection.

An expert on Civil War photography reviewed the prints and determined that the chest held one of the nation's finest collections of Civil War pictures, with many of the images unpublished or previously unknown to scholars. The collection had been assembled late in the nineteenth century by a former Medford mayor, General Samuel Crocker Lawrence, who served as commander of the Lawrence Light Guard during the war. After Lawrence's death in 1911, the collection passed into the hands of the Light Guard and, in 1948, the unit's commander gave the prints to the Medford Historical Society where they were relegated to storage and obscurity.

News of this "discovery" (including major newspaper coverage and an announcement in the *Civil War Times, Illustrated*) spread rapidly among Civil War historians and enthusiasts. Gordon Baldwin of the Getty Museum, one of the scholars who initially examined the images, noted that "the Medford hoard of photographs is without doubt one of the most important collections in this country of prints made from the original negatives of some of the most important photographers of the Civil War." Overrun by numerous requests to see or purchase the photographs by persons from all walks of life, the Society moved the prints to a bank vault, limited access to a small number of accredited scholars, and embarked upon a comprehensive program of conservation and restoration. That process continues and the collection is still unavailable. This book, which contains selected examples of the collection, constitutes the first public presentation of these images. The Society hopes that funds generated by this volume will help underwrite the remainder of the conservation effort.

The editor selected images for inclusion in the book because of individual aesthetic quality rather than for historical comprehensiveness. The photographs selected, however, do provide a general chronological representation of the war from Fort Sumter to views of a devastated Richmond. There are images of Union encampments around Washington, D.C., the Chattanooga campaign of 1863, Gettysburg, and Sherman's march to the sea. The book contains almost 100 images, with about three-quarters of them full-page plates. There are two rather spectacular fold-out pages which provide panoramic views of cavalry stables near Washington, D.C. and of the bomb-blasted Gallego Flour Mills in Virginia. Each of the plates in the volume is introduced by a short paragraph describing the location, event, person, or subject depicted while, in many cases, research has identified the photographer.

Although most of the photographs in the volume are previously unpublished, informed students of the Civil War probably will not find astonishing revelations of heretofore unphotographed subjects, events, or topics. Such is due, however, to the nature of Civil War photography and not to shortcomings in this volume or the Medford Collection. There were a relatively small number of Civil War photographers, with the majority of them working on the Union side. These included Alexander Gardner, Timothy O'Sullivan, George N. Barnard, and Andrew J. Russell. They operated mostly in the Eastern Theater, usually based in Washington D.C. or traveling with one of the major Union armies in Virginia, Maryland, Tennessee, or Georgia. Images by these Union photographers understandably predominate in the Medford Collection. Since these photographers could be in only so many places at a given time and tended to be repetitious in themes and subjects, many prints in the Medford Collection apparently mirror those in other archival and photographic holdings.

Moreover, the cumbersome technology and heavy photographic equipment of the time made action-based images impossible, so the majority of Civil War photographs consist of behind-the-lines images of supply depots, hospitals, staging areas, and "aftermath" views of major battles fought mostly east of the Appalachians. This is true for the Medford Collection. Additionally, given the sentiments of nineteenth-century romanticism, most Civil War photographers delighted in posing their subjects and artificially staging their images without regard to our modern sensibilities of journalistic accuracy. As well, since these photographers were civilians who took pictures primarily to make money, they specialized in taking formal *carte de visite* portraits of individuals or small groups of people which they then sold to their subjects. These latter images of particular persons, many of whom are today unknown to history, survived by the tens of thousands and large numbers of them are scattered in archives throughout the nation, including the trunk at Medford.

Although dealing with typical or previously-photographed subjects, the Medford images are unique because many of them provide different views or new perspectives of particular events or incidents depicted in already-known photographs. Alexander Gardner, for example, dragged the corpse of a young soldier some forty yards from where it fell at Devil's Den, posed it to his satisfaction, and then snapped one of the most compelling images of the war, long-known as the "Gettysburg Sharpshooter." The Medford Collection contains a Gardner picture taken before he moved the young man's body and made the well-known photograph. In addition, there are new views of the dedication ceremony at the Gettysburg Cemetery, including a crowd scene which shows the speaker's platform in the distance. Rounding out the volume, the book also contains a few photographs published in nineteenth-century compilations because the Medford Collection contains high-quality prints of them, with scenes of William T. Sherman in Georgia predominating in this category.

When made available to the public, the Medford Collection will enrich the nation's stock of Civil War images greatly, but it will probably do so without altering or revising current views of the conflict as reflected in the photographic record. This same point can be made about the volume under review. It provides new, compelling, and meaningful images of the war. For that reason alone, it belongs in the hands of every person interested in the history of the Civil War. Beyond that, however, this book contributes little more understanding for the modern reader than already can be found in such pictorial compilations as William C. Davis' *Shadows of the Storm,* Paul Angle's *A Pictorial History of the Civil War,* the reprint of George N. Barnard's *Photographic Views of Sherman's Campaign,* and other standard works dealing with Civil War photography. Nonetheless, that fact does not contradict the importance of the Medford Collection as a valuable historical source or of this volume's significance. It constitutes a welcome addition to the history of Civil War photography.

LIGHT TOWNSEND CUMMINS
AUSTIN COLLEGE

Holding the Line, by Flavel C. Barber edited by Robert H. Ferrell (The Kent State University Press, P.O. Box 5190, Kent, Ohio 44242-0001) 1994. B&W photos, epilogue, appendix, notes, bibliography, index. 281pp. Cloth. $28.00

Flavel C. Barber's *Holding the Line: The Third Tennessee Infantry. 1861-1864* tells the story of a Confederate regiment that was captured at Fort Donelson, Tennessee, successfully defended Chickasaw Bayou, Mississippi, and saw its last action at Resaca, Georgia. That Barber actually fought with the Third Tennessee makes the book a rarity, gives his prose the engaging quality of a firsthand report, and makes it a pleasure to read. Robert H. Ferrell, Distinguished Professor Emeritus of History at Indiana University, edited Barber's work. Ferrell writes that Barber's excellent prose made his job easy, but he put substantial effort into compiling the appendix, a roster of the Third Tennessee, and excellent explanatory notes that readers must not skip if they hope to get a full appreciation of the Third's story.

Barber began life in Union County, Pennsylvania, but moved to Tennessee while still a young man. He attended college there and by 1860 had become a successful farmer and teacher in Giles County. When the war broke out, he helped raise a company of what would become the Third Tennessee, and was married the evening before departing as a captain with the company for training and action. Barber used his teacher's eye and literary skills to record his wartime experiences. Ferrell weeded out what he felt were "humdrum" portions of Barber's account and began the book's narrative with the regiment's participation in the battle at Fort Donelson. From that point Ferrell weaves together Barber's record, sometimes in the form of diary entries and other times in the form of narratives addressing periods of intense activity written by Barber during his captivity or other less busy periods.

Immediately Barber plunges the reader into the hell of war. Bullets, balls, and grapeshot fill the air around the Third Tennessee, shattering trees and human bones indiscriminately. Union forces captured the regiment, which Barber blames on the inefficiency of Confederate field officers who had lost the respect of their men.

The misery of battle thus gives way to the humiliation of surrender, which Barber depicts as an exercise in chaos, fear, and severe disappointment. Remarkably, given the passionate emotions he must have experienced, Barber maintains an even hand in discussing captivity and his captors. He acknowledges good among Union soldiers when he sees it and criticizes brutality when he sees that. He retains this objectivity throughout.

The shift from battlefield to prisoner of war camp takes the reader by surprise. The regiment trades periods of intense activity, excitement, and danger on the battlefield for the grinding monotony of prison life. Barber served time in Camp Chase, near Columbus, Ohio, and then on Johnson's Island, a prison camp in Sandusky Bay in Lake Erie. Eating became the prisoners' chief preoccupation. Newspapers provided hours of diversion daily. Prized letters from home were read again and again. As in his battlefield depictions, Barber successfully brings the reader into his world as a prisoner.

Probably the most significant contribution Barber makes to Civil War literature comes in his story of the Battle of Chickasaw Bayou, located just outside Vicksburg, in December 1862. Here a Confederate force, considerably outnumbered by Union troops under Maj. Gen. William T. Sherman, defeated their opponents soundly. Previous accounts spread credit for the Confederate victory to a number of units. Barber's account suggests that the Third Tennessee turned away Sherman's forces practically single-handedly, thanks in part to their holding a nearly impregnable position.

About midway, the book becomes mostly diary entries. Although these offer valuable insights into life in a Confederate infantry unit, they do not read as well as the portions presented as narrative. Typically they offer comments on the weather and the given day's significant activities, which in many cases were not particularly significant.

Barber, by then promoted to major, fought his last battle defending Resaca, Georgia. He died there after being shot while leading a charge on May 14, 1864. His last words expressed confidence that the Third Tennessee would continue to do its duty. The unit fulfilled his confidence by fighting nearly a year after his death before surrendering on April 26, 1865.

Although Ferrell produced an eminently readable version of Barber's record, Barber's objectivity leaves the reader wanting more at times. How did Barber, as a transplanted Pennsylvanian, feel about the war, for instance? Did not the war stir wild emotions in the man? If so, he has removed most of their traces. In that sense, he represents a quintessential example of the Victorian model for male behavior, constantly in command of his emotions and never revealing their unseemly side.

Overall, Ferrell and Barber achieve a significant success. The book informs on life in a Confederate infantry unit under a variety of circumstances and gives glimpses into the daily lives of its officers. Congratulations to Ferrell and the Kent State University Press for including excellent maps, illustrations, and photographs, including a wonderful portrait of Barber. Make room on the shelf for this fine volume.

TODD KERSTETTER

UNIVERSITY OF NEBRASKA

More Generals In Gray by Bruce S. Allardice (Louisiana State University Press, Baton Rouge, LA 70803) 1995. 300pp. Bibliography. Cloth. $29.95.

Military historians pursuing information about a particular Confederate general usually consult Ezra Warner's *Generals in Gray: Lives of the Confederate Commanders,* or Mark M. Boatner III's *Civil War Dictionary.* These sources provide adequate information about regularly appointed generals, but offer either few or no facts about the many Confederates who served as generals without the benefit of an official appointment from President Jefferson Davis and later approval by the Confederate Congress. Bruce S. Allardice's work seeks to fill this information gap with brief articles about 137 men who served as generals without presidential appointments and Congressional confirmation.

Allardice's preface explains how Confederate law defined a general, the procedure for appointments and confirmation to the rank of general, and the criteria Allardice developed to select the men for examination in his book. The 137 men discussed in this work include soldiers that Lieutenant General Edmund Kirby Smith, commander of the Trans-Mississippi Department, promoted to the rank of general, men that the *Official Records* show as assigned to a general's rank, those viewed by contemporaries as generals though there is no official documentation of their appointment, generals in "one of the state armies organized in 1861" (p. 12), state militia generals who led their troops in a campaign, or one of five men (including Henry Kyd Douglas) that modern works often mention as generals but were "only occasionally called general by contemporaries" (p.12).

The body of the work consists of short articles about these "other" Confederate generals arranged alphabetically by surname. Most of the articles are between one page and one-and-a-half pages in length and contain valuable information such as birth data, names of parents, pre-war career, war service, postwar career (if any), and an evaluation of the soldier's claim to the rank of general. Following each article is a helpful short bibliography of sources. Louisiana State University Press will include photographs for 108 men in the finished text, but this reviewer was unable to comment on photographic quality since L. S. U. included no photographs in the advance uncorrected proof sent for review.

The variety of people discussed in this work and the colorful lives of many of them encourages the reader to browse. William Bartee Wade, for example, shot seven occupation soldiers in 1866 before being wounded and carried to a local hotel. Three days later, soldiers removed the recuperating Wade from his bed and murdered him by throwing him out of an upper story window. John Robert Baylor of Texas possessed a "ferocious temper" (p. 33), and secretive Colton Greene of Missouri hid most facts about his ante-bellum life. Several entries detail the lives of men who compiled impressive combat records. These notables include Raphael Semmes, the famed commander of the *CSS Alabama,* James Hagan, who survived three wounds as he led his troops through the campaigns of the Army of Tennessee, and Meriwether "Jeff" Thompson, the famed "Swamp Fox" of the Trans-Mississippi. In addition, Allardice provides articles about Jeffrey E. Forrest, a fine officer and a younger brother of Lieutenant General Nathan Bedford Forrest, and George Washington Rains, who constructed the impressive gunpowder factory in Augusta, Georgia.

Following the body of the work is an appendix and a bibliography. The appendix consists of brief entries about 135 additional men whose claims as general are less reliable. Many of these footnoted entries refer to state militia officers or men who simply assumed the title of general after the war. Allardice's bibliography reveals the impressive depth of research necessary to compile this book. Allardice effectively used many primary sources such as burial records, city directories, compiled service records, court records, family papers, genealogies, and newspapers to write about his often elusive subjects.

More Generals in Gray is a fine, well-organized, well-researched work that presents information about many men who contributed significantly to the Confederate war effort. This work includes articles about generals from all theatres of the war, but those who served in the western theatre or the Trans-Mississippi theatre are particularly well-represented. *More Generals in Gray* belongs on your Civil War reference shelf as a worthy companion volume to Ezra Warner's *Generals in Gray.*

M. JANE JOHANSSON
PRYOR, OK

The Capture of New Orleans, 1862, Chester G. Hearn (Louisiana State University Press, Baton Rouge, LA 70893) 1995. B&W photos, introduction, epilogue, appendix, bibliography, index. 292pp. Cloth. $26.95.

Any individual who has read so little as a one-volume general survey on the American Civil War probably would pose this question to themselves, if not to more knowledgeable experts: how could Confederate authorities, civil, military, or naval, have been so short sighted as to allow New Orleans, their most populous and wealthiest city, the entrepot and egress point of its most important waterway and trade network, the Lower Mississippi, to fall to Union naval and military forces within a year after the firing on Fort Sumter? Multiple causation theories have been advanced, villains and heroes identified, and both Confederate and Union positions and strategies rationalized. However, for the first time in a long while, an effort to unravel the extremely complicated web of the capture of New Orleans—with perspectives from both sides—has been undertaken.

While the reader will find the book disjointed in places, time sequences convoluted, and the narrative threads occasionally puzzling, Hearn should be given credit for his workmanlike effort in attempting to clarify the often anachronistic positions taken by both sides. Confederate leaders, civil, military, and naval, especially, never adequately determined whose responsibility it was to defend the Crescent City from attack. Indeed, they could never determine, until it was too late, which direction, above or below, posed the greatest threat. It was their miscalculation that the greatest threat lay from the upper reaches of the Mississippi. The path upriver from the Gulf was thought to be virtually impregnable, with the cross-firing batteries of Fort Jackson and Fort St. Philip, the chain and derelict barrier stretched across the River, and the shifting bars of the River's multiple passes which would prohibit deep draft vessels from reaching the Head of the Passes. This sense that the city was invulnerable from the Gulf approaches contributed to the City's fall in April 6, 1862.

General Mansfield Lovell, northern-born but Confederate, and in charge of the military defense of the city, became a natural target for opprobrium. Confederate President Jefferson Davis' unwillingness to concede his own negligence in the fall of New Orleans contains a degree of irony because Davis and his brother Joseph's holdings, located along the banks of the Big Muddy, utilized both the river and New Orleans as the outlet for their cotton trade and the entrepot for import abroad. He remained perfectly content, even after the conflict, to let Lovell bear the blame, even though every time Lovell organized a formidable defense force for New Orleans, Davis allowed the Confederate War Department to strip it from the city and dispatch it elsewhere for Confederate service. Consequently, when the final showdown came, Lovell had little more than an ill-equipped token force to face Union Gen. Benjamin F. Butler's 15.000-man army. Neither does Davis take into account the fourteen vessels of Captain David G. Farragut that could have used the streets of New Orleans—running from the river, which was at high-water stage—as open fields of fire. Surely, Davis, in his post-bellum memoirs, should have been more charitable toward Lovell, and more willing to accept, at least partially, responsibility for the debacle in the West, the very section of the Confederacy from which he hailed and best appreciated.

Although unstated specifically, the failure of Confederate nationalism can be discerned in the actions of Secretary of the Navy Stephen R. Mallory of Florida, who had to reconcile differences as well as chains of command between the Confederate Mosquito Fleet, vessels belonging to the State of Louisiana placed under Confederate authority, the River Defense Fleet, ostensibly under the control of the War Department, and private entrepreneurs who secured contracts to build the ironclads for the defense of the Crescent City. The reviewer sees additional irony in that President Davis' initial choice for secretary of the navy was Louisianian John J. Perkins, Jr., but, since Louisiana had already secured a cabinet position in Judah P. Benjamin, state's rights doctrine dictated that cabinet posts be represented by different states. Perkins, a member of the Confederate Congress, would have been more attuned to the significance of defending New Orleans and the Mississippi River in order to maintain the Trans-Mississippi West as an integral part of the supply line to the eastern and western theatre of conflict. However, Mallory should be credited with producing a formidable deepwater and riverine Confederate Navy from scratch. Given the limited financial capital, maritime expertise, and industrial resources of the 11 Confederate states, perhaps Mallory endeavored to accomplish too much with the limited resources available to him. An excellent case in point was Mallory's signing two contracts, one with E. C. Murray to build the ironclad *Louisiana*, and another with Nelson and Asa F. Tift to build the ironclad *Mississippi*. Eventually Murray and the Tifts shared the same tract, operating separate shipyards on adjoining lots north of New Orleans in Jefferson City. Even a cursory examination of the evidence in reference to availability of iron, building materials, engines, propellers, and cannon, as well as the presence of an adequate number of ship carpenters, reveals too much duplication of effort. Only the *Louisiana* was outfitted to be present, but ineffective, when Farragut's fleet ran the forts. Certainly, the vague chain of command and lack of cooperation between the Confederate army and navy authorities contributed significantly to the loss of New Orleans.

The Union had a navy with an intact command structure when secession occurred, and President Abraham Lincoln fortunately enlisted the aid of two extremely competent individuals, Gideon Welles as secretary of the navy and Gustavus V. Fox as assistant secretary of the navy, whose talents complemented each other rather than detracted from the Navy's mission. The selection of southern born Captain David G. Farragut to lead the Union fleet upriver proved a significant decision. Farragut, an adopted brother of David Dixon Porter, both of whom were familiar with the lower course of the river, afforded a positive degree of cooperation between the two siblings in spite of Porter's ambitions for promotion. Quite insightful are Hearn's conclusions on the disparate element in the Union's strategy equation, the personality clashes within the ranks of the Navy, as well as the inter-service rivalry. Although Farragut remained aloof from the personality conflicts, the politically influential General Butler and the commander of the mortar squadron, Porter, remained protagonists even after the War. Indeed, the ambitious Porter dispatched reports to Assistant Secretary Fox that enhanced his own importance, even at the expense of his adopted brother, and certainly was detracting toward any naval or army officer whose views conflicted with his own perceptions. Hearn analyzes dutifully the composition of the Federal fleet as well as Porter's bomb-boat squadron. His descriptions of the actions of individual Federal vessels in passing Fort Jackson and Fort St. Philip and the Confederate defense are quite cogent, and among the best this reviewer has read in a secondary source.

The actual surrender of New Orleans is only briefly sketched after Farragut's fleet has reached the Head of the Passes and run the gauntlet of both forts' cannon, the barrier across the River. The arrival of his 14 vessels at Quarantine essentially marked the end of organized Confederate resistance.

Hearn meticulously mined almost every reference to the campaign found in the *War of the Rebellion* and the *Naval War Records*, and supplemented that with primary manuscript sources and published primary sources, including newspapers, and secondary references. He might have been able to personalize his narrative with excerpts from the *Confederate Veteran* or *Union Loyal League* publications. The microfilmed "Captured Rebel Archives for Louisiana" may contain more details on the State of Louisiana's efforts to defend New Orleans. This reviewer, however, intends to keep this monograph nearby as a ready reference on the riverine war along the lower Mississippi. Hearn has brought a semblance of reasonable order to a very convoluted campaign.

MARSHALL SCOTT LEGAN
NORTHEAST LOUISIANA UNIVERSITY

April '65: Confederate Covert Action in the American Civil War by William A. Tidwell (The Kent State University Press, P. O. Box 5190, Kent, Ohio 44242-0001) 1995. Notes, bibliography, index. 264pp. Cloth. $30.00

April '65 is William A. Tidwell's companion book to his *Come Retribution: The Confederate Secret Service and the Assassination of Lincoln* (1988), with James O. Hall and David Winfred Gaddy. *Come Retribution* marked an important milestone in the historiography of the Confederate Secret Service and the assassination of President Abraham Lincoln.

Over the years, researchers and others have proposed various theories about the assassination of President Lincoln. Immediately after his assassination, in April 1865, the federal government began to assemble its case against the suspected conspirators. Federal prosecutors tried to tie the assassination to the Confederate government, but for various reasons were unsuccessful. In the postwar period, Southerners successfully contended that actor John Wilkes Booth acted alone in his "mad" plot to kill Lincoln. In 1937 Otto Eisenschiml argued that Secretary of War Edwin M. Stanton and a group of northern businessmen had conspired to murder Lincoln. The Eisenschiml theory caught the fancy of the American public in spite of its flawed logic. In *The Lincoln Murder Conspiracies*, William Hanchett delivered serious blows to Eisenschiml's theory and opened the way for the development of a new one. In 1988 the publication of *Come Retribution* brought the Lincoln murder theories full circle by again proposing a link between the Confederate government and the assassination. *Come Retribution* detailed the recruitment of Booth by the Confederate Secret Service, the plot to kidnap Lincoln and its failure, the creation of an escape route through Maryland, a failed plan to bomb the White House in April 1865 as General Robert E. Lee planned to evacuate Richmond, Virginia, and the later decision by Booth to disrupt the federal government by killing Lincoln, Vice-President Andrew Johnson, and Secretary of State William H. Seward. *April '65* is Tidwell's attempt to present additional evidence in support of the basic thesis presented in *Come Retribution*. For instance, *April '65* seeks to address reviewers' criticisms that *Come Retribution* failed to prove the existence of an "active secret service" (p. 11) or the identity of the person who ordered the bombing of the White House.

The main title, *April '65*, is somewhat misleading since it implies that the major purpose of the work is to discuss the events of that month, including the Lincoln assassination. Although the discussion of Lincoln's murder is a major theme, most of the book deals with proving that the Confederate Secret Service was capable of developing a kidnapping scheme and a plan to bomb the White House. Tidwell's illumination of this murky world is interesting, startling, and convincing. Tidwell contends that the Confederate Secret Service, although small by modern standards, was creative and flexible, although loosely organized and made up of several different bureaus. According to Tidwell, the most important parts of the Secret Service were special cavalry scouts, the Greenhow Group, the Navy Submarine Battery Service, the Provost Marshall of Richmond, Secret Service operations in Canada, the State Department's Secret Service, the War Department's Secret Service, Signal Bureau and Signal Corps, Torpedo Bureau, and Strategy Bureau.

Tidwell includes several pages on each of these and devotes a chapter each to the Greenhow Group and the Canadian operations. Tidwell also includes a chapter about the fascinating character Bernard Janin Sage, who proposed ideas concerning privateering, a volunteer navy, and creating groups of "destructionists" trained to destroy Union supply depots, gunboats, transports, and other property. The Confederacy implemented many of Sage's ideas.

Tidwell is less successful at proving conclusively who ordered the bombing of the White House. By studying expenditures for Secret Service activities and detailing the procedure for drawing money from the Confederate Treasury, Tidwell argues that President Jefferson Davis approved of the operation and gave the final authorization for it.

April '65 is an important piece of detective work. Tidwell's personal background as a former member of military intelligence and later of the Central Intelligence Agency enables him to bring a different and important perspective to the Lincoln assassination and the Confederate Secret Service. The chapters about the Secret Service are particularly intriguing and hopefully will encourage scholars to further investigate this neglected area. Tidwell's work, although a fairly small volume, is packed with detail and may appeal primarily to the specialist rather than the general reader. Those interested in the Lincoln assassination and the Confederate Secret service will learn a great deal from this provocative work.

M. JANE JOHANSSON
PRYOR, OK

Medical Histories of Confederate Generals, by Jack D. Welsh (The Kent State University Press, P.O. Box 5190, Kent, Ohio 44242-0001) 1995. Bibliography. 297pp. Cloth. $ 35.00

Just as Ezra Warner was inspired to write *Generals in Gray* after reading Douglas Southall Freeman's *Lee's Lieutenants,* so was Jack Welsh inspired by reading the same three famous volumes to write *Medical Histories of Confederate Generals.*

Because Dr. Welsh is a lifelong practicing physician and an Emeritus Professor at the University of Oklahoma Health Science Center, he writes with the warm understanding and pathos of a dedicated physician. Equally importantly he researches and writes with the skill and expertise of a professor.

Dr. Welsh, in *Medical Histories*, has taken the same list of 425 Confederate generals found in Warner's book and has researched each one as to occupation, family, and medical history before, during, and after the Civil War. While reading straight through the book, this observer made a simple occupation survey and was astonished to find that in addition to the 146 West Point Graduates, there were 135 attorneys, eighteen planters, two politicians, twelve businessmen, ten teachers, and a smattering of other occupations.

Dr. Welsh has made no effort, when detailing various medical incidents, to infer any effect on the outcome of a battle or the war; neither has he made reference to heroism or the exact locations of a medical incident on the battlefield. Even so, one comes out of the pages in this book amazed at the devotion to duty of these generals in spite of wounds or illness.

While relishing references to the Civil War vintage diagnoses and treatments related in the book and in the unique eighteen-page glossary, one remembers that anesthesia was available, but no knowledge of germs existed during the great conflict.

Violence in pre-war years is notable in the lives of these generals. Pat Cleburne and Thomas Hindman were wounded in the same street fight. Wade Hampton and Ben McCullough bore scars from fighting bears with a knife. Twenty-nine were wounded in Mexico while six were wounded by Indian arrows. It is possible that a pre-war duel left nerve damage that prevented Albert Sidney Johnston from realizing that he was bleeding to death from his knee wound.

As if the rich medical histories and glossary were not enough, Dr. Welsh has provided a sixteen-page chronological sequence of medical events of the war.

In summary, before using the remaining space in giving the reader a few samples of individual histories, let it be said that Dr. Welsh has brought together in one fine volume an outstanding source of research material. Every Civil War speaker, every biographer, and every library with any coverage of the Great Conflict must have this book. Patrick Ronayne Cleburne, page 40: " On may 24, 1856, Cleburne was shot in the back during a street fight. Before collapsing he shot one of his attackers. He was carried across the street to a building. Blood streamed from his mouth, his eyes were glassy, and his breathing faint. The bullet had hit Cleburne three inches above the crest of the ileum to the right of the spine. It traveled upward at a forty-five degree angle and finally lodged underneath the skin and rested on the ensiform (xiphoid) cartilage. Later the bullet was removed without anesthesia but for years he had fragile health. An hour's debate would cause his mouth to fill with blood. In 1862, he stopped to talk with Col. L. E. Polk and a ball passed through his left cheek, carried away some teeth and emerged from his open mouth. A few weeks later he was back on the field.

At Perryville, in 1862, he was wounded near the ankle by a cannon shot that killed his horse but he remained in command. At the Battle of Franklin in 1864 while he was on foot, two horses having been shot from under him, he was killed when a minie ball entered his left abdomen."

Richard Brooke Garnett, page 76: "Late in June 1863, while ill with a fever, he was accidentally kicked in the ankle by a horse and had to travel in an ambulance. On July 3, while at Gettysburg, Garnett was too sick to walk, yet despite orders to the contrary, he insisted on leading the charge of his brigade from horseback. It has been stated that he wore his old blue overcoat in spite of the fact that it was a very hot day. Instead, he probably wore a new gray uniform that he had purchased in Richmond two weeks earlier. Garnett was hit in the head by a rifle ball and fell dead from his horse during the assault on Cemetery Hill. Other reports say that he was killed by grapeshot and almost cut in half. He had been riding to the rear of his advancing line, trying to keep it closed. When he was shot, he was within twenty-five paces of the stone wall."

John Brown Gordon, page 83: "At Sharpsburg, in 1862, Gordon was wounded five times. First he was shot through the calf of the right leg, then he was hit higher up in the same leg, but as he suffered no broken bones, he was able to continue on the field encouraging his men. Later in the day, a ball pierced his left arm and tore the tendons and flesh, but he remained on the field, blood running down his fingers. A fourth ball ripped through his shoulder, leaving a wad of clothing in the wound. Gordon still stayed on the field although weak from blood loss and scarcely able to stand. After he had gone only a short distance, he was struck in the face by a ball, which just missed the jugular vein when it passed out. Speaking of his wound after the war, Gordon said that it felt as if the top of his head was gone and that only a part of one jaw along with part of his tongue was left. The wounds were complicated by erysipelas and his wife nursed him back to health. His face was not healed when he returned to duty and was promoted to brigadier in

November 1862. Near Shepherdstown, he was wounded over the right eye, had the wound bandaged and returned to the field in thirty minutes. After Appomattox Courthouse, he became a U. S. Senator from Georgia and Governor."

These samples represent only a minute taste of the courage, character, and dedication of the Confederate Generals in the war.

WAYMON B. NORMAN, M.D.
LONGVIEW, TX

Index

CIVIL WAR REGIMENTS BACK ISSUES

See page iii for ordering information under the heading:

"SUBSCRIPTIONS, BACK ISSUES, COLLECTOR'S SETS"

THE CIVIL WAR IS ON-LINE

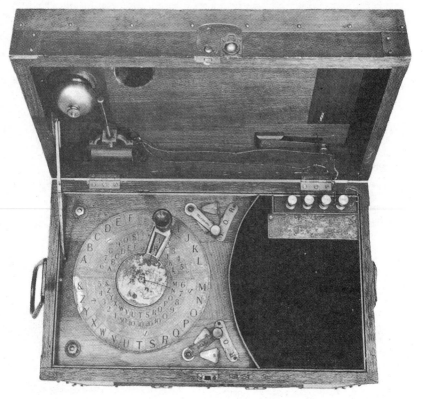

One of the Beardslee magneto-electric telegraph units used by the Union Signal Corps (Smithsonian Institution)

COMPUSERVE'S CIVIL WAR FORUM is a friendly and informative community of historians and buffs who daily discuss a broad array of topics related to the Civil War era. It is an electronic Civil War Round Table— a well organized and moderated on-line venue—with members from around the nation and many foreign countries.

Message sections and rapidly expanding libraries feature such categories as BATTLES/CAMPAIGNS, CIVIL WAR ART AND COLLECTIBLES, UNIT HISTORIES, RESEARCH RESOURCES, VISITING THE BATTLEFIELDS, and more. Our bi-monthly live conferences are one-hour Q&A sessions with people who have made a mark in the area of Civil War studies. The conference series was inaugurated in May by James McPherson and Steven Woodworth, followed in June by Michael Musick (June 6) and Edwin C. Bearss (June 20). Drop by the forum for an expanded conference schedule, or download transcripts of these conversations from the forum library.

To access the COMPUSERVE CIVIL WAR FORUM, type "GO CIVILWAR" at any Compuserve prompt. If you are not a member of Compuserve, or wish to receive more information, contact David Woodbury, Forum SysOp, at 76710.261@compuserve.com. For a free CIS software kit, call (800) 487-0453.

LSU Press

A Mississippi Rebel in the Army of Northern Virginia
The Civil War Memoirs of Private David Holt

Edited by Thomas D. Cockrell and Michael B. Ballard

"Holt offers an engaging glimpse of the 16th Mississippi Infantry far from home, bleeding on the battlefields of Shenandoah, Chancellorsville, Gettysburg and more. His narrative is inventive, colorful, and unfailingly engaging."

—**William C. Davis**, author of *Jefferson Davis: The Man and His Hour*

Illustrated
$34.95

The Louisiana Native Guards
The Black Military Experience During the Civil War

James G. Hollandsworth, Jr.

"This was a regiment only Louisiana could have produced, and in the end, a telling measure of what the war was about."

—**David W. Blight**, author of *Frederick Douglass' Civil War*

Illustrated
$24.95

New Paperbacks

The March to the Sea and Beyond
Sherman's Troops in the Savannah and Carolinas Campaigns

Joseph T. Glatthaar

Winner of the Bell Irvin Wiley Award, the Fletcher Pratt Award, and the Jefferson Davis Award

"Their competence, their intelligence, their dedication shine all through Glatthaar's pages."

—***Journal of Southern History***

$14.95 paper

Out of the Storm
The End of the Civil War, April–June 1865

Noah Andre Trudeau

"Superb and important—another groundbreaking achievement in research and narration for Trudeau, covering a period not often examined in depth by Civil War historians."

—***Booklist*** (starred review)

Illustrated
$16.95 paper

Colonel Grenfell's Wars
The Life of a Soldier of Fortune

Stephen Z. Starr

"All Grenfell has lacked is a biographer and now he has found one. Stephen Starr is obviously fascinated with his subject and he transmits his fascination to the reader."

—***Virginia Quarterly Review***

$14.95 paper